Action Research
in the Classroom

Vivienne Baumfield, Elaine Hall and Kate Wall

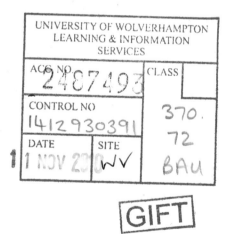

Los Angeles • London • New Delhi • Singapore

SAGE Publications Ltd
1 Oliver's Yard
55 City Road
London EC1Y 1SP

SAGE Publications Inc.
2455 Teller Road
Thousand Oaks, California 91320

SAGE Publications India Pvt Ltd
B 1/I 1 Mohan Cooperative Industrial Area
Mathura Road
New Delhi 110 044

SAGE Publications Asia-Pacific Pte Ltd
33 Pekin Street #02-01
Far East Square
Singapore 048763

Library of Congress Control Number: 2007930359

British Library Cataloguing in Publication data

A catalogue record for this book is available from the British Library

ISBN 978-1-4129-3039-0
ISBN 978-1-4129-3040-6 (pbk)

Typeset by C&M Digitals (P) Ltd., Chennai, India
Printed in Great Britain by The Cromwell Press, Trowbridge, Wiltshire
Printed on paper from sustainable resources

07/08

UNIVERSITY OF WOLVERHAMPTON

Harrison Learning Centre
City Campus
University of Wolverhampton
St Peter's Square
Wolverhampton WV1 1RH
Telephone: 0845 408 1631

2 8 JAN 2011

Ac

Telephone Renewals: 01902 321333 or 0845 408 1631
Please Return this item on or before the last date shown above.
Fines will be charged if items are returned late.
See tariff of fines displayed at the Counter.

Contents

Acknowledgements

The authors would like to extend their thanks to the many people who have contributed to this book.

To our editor, Patrick Brindle, for his enthusiasm and support.

To our colleagues in various institutions, past and present, who have shared ideas and challenged our thinking. To colleagues in the Research Centre for Learning and Teaching at Newcastle University for their encouragement and support. In particular to David Leat, Jo McShane and Karen Lowing who have read draft chapters and commented on them and to Steve Higgins, who has done all of the above and much more.

To all of the organisations, teachers, researchers and students who generously allowed us to use their research data in the chapters:

Stella Onwuemene, Aylward High School, Enfield
John Welham, Camborne Science and Community College, Cornwall
Linda Siegle and Rebecca Goodbourn at the Campaign for Learning
John Rutter, Ellesmere Port Specialist School for Performing Arts, Cheshire
Jane Gormally, Francis Power and Caroline Wood, Fallibroome High School, Cheshire
Emma Glasner and Ulfet Mahmout, Fleecefield Primary School, Enfield
Staff from Greenfields Nursery, North Tyneside
Laurel Barber, Hazlebury Infant School, Enfield
Ann Dutoy, Henbury High School, Cheshire
Helen Burrell, High Spen Primary School, Gateshead
Karen Brooker, Kehelland Primary School, Cornwall
Pipper Pender and Liz Martin, Lanner Primary School, Cornwall
Shelley Long, Kathy Heap and Leaf Lane Primary School, Cheshire
Neera Jobanputra, Newcastle University
Heather Smith, Newcastle University
Sandra Sefer, Oakthorpe Primary School, Enfield
Nicola Furnish and Helen Tonkin, Pennoweth Primary School, Cornwall
Karen Steadman, Raynham Primary School, Enfield
Mandi Horwood and Erica Morgan, The Roseland School, Cornwall
Linda Stephens and Irene Pooley, St Meriadoc Primary School, Cornwall
Robert Peers, Ann D'Echevairra, Jo Bowden and colleagues at the Thinking for Learning Unit, Northumberland

Pat Williams and Ann Webb, Treloweth Primary School, Cornwall
Michelle Eathorne, Treviglas High School, Cornwall
Karleen Ovenden, Walker Technology College, Newcastle
Ann Mulcahy and Elaine Saini, Wilbury Primary School, Enfield
Vicky Lewis and Helen Barwick, Winsford High Street Primary School, Cheshire

We would like to commemorate the life and work of Marie Butterworth who did so much to develop teacher research in her own school and beyond and who died before this book was published.

And to all the teacher-researchers we have worked with over the years who have provided the inspiration and impetus for our work.

List of Figures and Tables

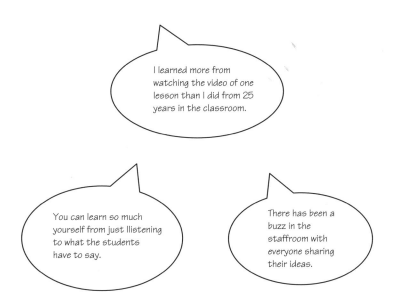

1

Creating and Translating Knowledge about Teaching and Learning

CHAPTER CONTENTS

- How can teacher enquiry develop knowledge about teaching and learning?
- What is the link between teacher enquiry and action research?
- Does working in collaborative partnerships support the sharing of knowledge about teaching and learning?

> I learned more from watching the video of one lesson than I did from 25 years in the classroom.

> You can learn so much yourself from just listening to what the students have to say.

> There has been a buzz in the staffroom with everyone sharing their ideas.

This book is about teachers as learners, finding out more about what is happening in their classrooms and contributing to our understanding of the processes of teaching and learning in today's schools. It is also about developing partnerships between teachers and university researchers in which distinctions between theory and practice are challenged and expertise is distributed as we learn together.

The suggestions, advice and practical tools included in this book have been developed through over ten years of collaboration with teachers investigating different aspects of learning across all phases of schooling from the foundation stage to the sixth form. Our work has been with teachers and students in Initial Teacher Education working in the education system in England and is grounded in that experience, but we have also been able to share what we have learned with people working in other education systems who are interested in enquiring into their practice. Our intention in writing this book is to provide a record of what we have learned together through a series of enquiries and as such it is both a guide to how an enquiry might be conducted and also a reflection on the processes.

Trying to present some ideas for teachers beginning to enquire into what is happening in their classrooms whilst also making reference to different forms of action research and the place of teacher enquiry within education research could result in this book falling between two stools. It is our hope that the book functions more as a rope bridge connecting the practice of teacher enquiry with the wider debate on the creation and translation of knowledge about teaching and learning. The analogy conveys the sense of improvisation, provisionality and risk that we believe to be an integral part of our work in learning together across different institutional contexts. We have included case studies written by teachers as illustrations of how tools have actually been used and issues tackled in classrooms. We also provide suggestions for further reading that include references to contrasting perspectives on teacher enquiry, action research and the use of methods beyond the scope of this introductory book.

Teacher enquiry

During the course of their careers teachers acquire a body of knowledge about teaching and learning which is shaped by their experiences in classrooms and their values about the purposes of education. Teachers are often unrecognised innovators and problem-solvers who take the raw materials of the curriculum and recommendations about good practice and adapt them to their personal and professional environments. This capacity to make adjustments is a recognised feature of not only the most effective teachers, but also of those who are most satisfied in their professional lives (Huberman, 2001; Hattie, 2003). However, the judgement regarding the 'best fit' of practice to context tends to be intuitive, based on an absence of negative feedback and sensitive to considerations of time and resources. As such, it has been described as tweaking or fine-tuning, as it has more of the characteristics of the way in which a craftsman develops and deploys expertise rather than those of a professional (Hargreaves, 1999; Huberman, 2001). In this book we begin to explore what happens when teachers engage in more sustained, explicit processes of enquiry in their classrooms and the extent to which a more robust body of professional knowledge can be shared across specific contexts is possible.

The evidence provided is not incontrovertible but, clearly, there is a good chance that a successful change to the Year 3 geography curriculum, focusing on peer talk and collaboration (for example) might work again next year, even though the children in the class will be different. However, the Year 3 teacher has changed, simply by being involved in the enquiry: her perspective on geography teaching has shifted. She wonders, will it work in maths? The group she teaches in maths is a lower-ability set – will that be a factor? The evidence generated by a single cycle of enquiry is the raw material for generating the next series of questions, so action research is conceptualised as a series of linked enquiries. Just as learning is an ongoing process, which builds and develops from experience and need, so enquiry can transform not just the practice of teachers, but their understanding of that practice and give them a range of tools for reflection and self-evaluation.

The relationship between research, policy and practice in the production and deployment of knowledge about teaching and learning is complex and subject to critique (Hammersley, 2005). Nevertheless, current conceptions of teaching as a profession – such as the new standards for teachers (Training and Development Agency, 2006) – assume that a productive relationship between these aspects is both possible and desirable, although they are often vague as to the exact nature of the dynamic involved. Figure 1.1 indicates how different types of research in education might interrelate with these domains. Our principal concern is with the interaction of theory and practice in the engagement of teachers in research into teaching and learning in their own classrooms: the research engaged professional.

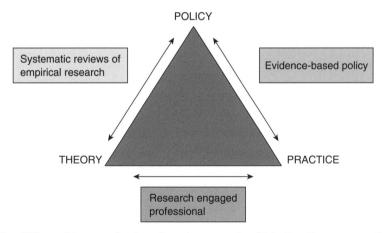

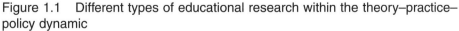

Figure 1.1   Different types of educational research within the theory–practice–policy dynamic

We want to know how teachers can be 'research engaged' in a way that is both manageable within their existing professional responsibilities and also sufficiently robust to effect real change. We look at how an enquiry approach can provide an evidence base that is not only relevant to the individual but which is shared. This sharing takes place over an expanding network from colleagues in school to a collaborative community of researching teachers and is subjected to scrutiny and validation. Participants contribute to a shared understanding of learning and teaching, including which things work within specific contexts, which elements are 'translatable' between contexts and which underpinning processes are common to learners.

Teacher enquiry and action research

So far we have been describing the process of research into practice in terms of teacher enquiry and it might be easier to continue to do so if it were not for the fact that we also draw upon aspects of action research. In the following section we offer a perspective on how we link teacher enquiry with action research in our work. We do so knowing that we run the risk of failing to satisfy those who are already familiar with the issues by saying too little, whilst distracting those who simply want to learn more about what we actually did. It is not the purpose of this book to add to the growing literature about action research but rather to provide an account of our collaboration with teachers to develop knowledge and understanding of pedagogy. Nevertheless, we recognise the need to acknowledge the wider debate and give some indication of where we position ourselves regarding the role of action research in the investigation of classroom practice. For those interested in pursuing this further we include references at the end of the chapter which engage with the issues in greater depth.

For the teachers, research is made manageable through two interrelated processes: the identification of the focus of the enquiry and the generation of questions and exploration through a cycle of action research. We believe that a cycle of action research fits alongside and is complementary to the model of *plan–do–review* underpinning teachers' practice (see Figure 1.2). As such, there is no requirement for the teachers to 'bolt on' or overlay another layer of 'research practices', rather they select research tools which fit with their teaching environment and use those to generate the necessary feedback in a systematic way; in this model of working it is only a short step from feedback that informs the next stage in the enquiry to evidence that is open to public scrutiny. Examples of case studies of the enquiries completed by teachers using this model are included in this book to illustrate how they have developed and customised research tools and approaches to meet the needs of their own contexts.

There are internal tensions in action research, which are best understood as opportunities for understanding and reflection about the enquiry. Whether they are consciously addressed or not, the variety of ways in which these tensions are resolved accounts for the diversity of projects under the 'action research umbrella' as the various re-combinations of DNA account for diversity in a species. For example, when surveying a group of cats, we will be aware that they have a number of core characteristics in common which identify their purpose and the way in which they operate – however, they also have a great many variations and adaptations to circumstance. Nevertheless, we recognise that a lynx, a tiger and a

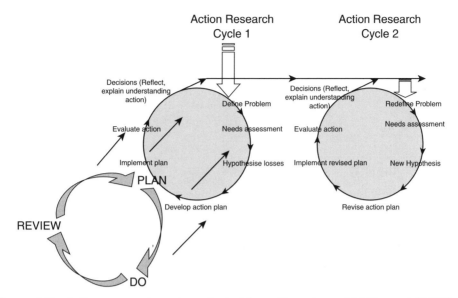

Figure 1.2   Action research cycles adapted from Kemmis and McTaggart (1988) as complementary to plan–do–review

tabby cat are similar enough to all be 'cats' and that there is no purpose in regarding tigers as inherently 'better' than lynx. What is interesting and useful is to explore what the differences between them mean for the way in which they operate in the world. So what are the key elements of action research which differentiate lynx, tigers and tabbies? Action research by definition requires purposeful enquiry into practices but the experience of individual researchers differs as the particular elements are combined.

Drawing on our experiences of working together on a number of projects with teachers we have constructed an understanding of action research that reflects the variety of practice but which is more than merely descriptive. We suggest that such understanding comes from the interrelations between three key aspects common to all research (see Figure 1.3):

1   the intention of the enquiry
2   the process by which the enquiry is pursued
3   the audience with which the enquiry is shared.

Intention

Agency

This refers to the extent to which the individual teacher-researcher has control of the focus of the enquiry, the methods used to pursue the project, the analysis and interpretation of data and the way in which the project is made public. In some research projects, one or more of these elements is controlled by other agents – a university research team, or senior managers at school or LEA level, for example.

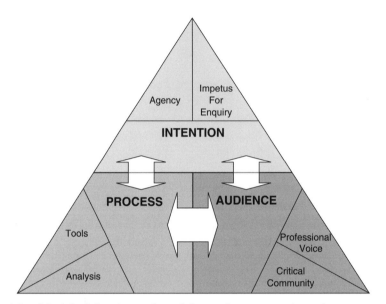

Figure 1.3   Model of the dynamics of the action research cycle

Impetus

The problem posed that stimulates the enquiry and provides the focus for the action research can come from a number of different sources: it can be an issue of concern at an individual teacher level, amongst a group of colleagues, across a whole school or group of schools. It can come from an experience in the classroom, from a question posed by an INSET session, a professional journal or from discussion with colleagues and managers. The impetus for the enquiry will have implications for the processes followed and the primary audience and have an effect on the dynamics of the action research cycle itself.

Process

Tools

This refers not simply to the research methods employed: the observations, questionnaires, interviews or test scores but the extent to which each method provides data which operates on more than one level. A pragmatic research tool simultaneously contributes to answering the research question and gives feedback information that enriches the learning and teaching in progress.

Analysis

The analytic process is one in which, broadly speaking, there is either a progressive narrowing of focus to assemble evidence to either prove or disprove a hypothesis or there is a broad mapping of the data collected in order to generate a rich description and a new hypothesis.

Audience

Voice   to spread widely

Dissemination is a key part of every project, but the extent to which it is prioritised reveals something important about the purpose of the enquiry as identified by the individual researcher. Is the intention to set in motion specific changes in pedagogy and practice, necessitating active dissemination well beyond the immediate environment, or to set up a ripple effect, whereby the impact of the research is most keenly felt in the immediate vicinity but may spread out through recommendation and colleagues' reports?

Critical community

This refers not just to the final presentation of results from an enquiry, but to how the researcher is placed in relation to others, from the initial idea, through the process of data collection, re-framing questions and analysing findings. This community may be other practitioners, other researchers or partners in universities. In terms of extremes on the continuum, there is at one end the 'lone' researcher, at the other, there is a formal team with clearly defined roles. However, the points of contact are important less for the number or the length of time, than for the extent to which they both support and challenge the researcher. The role of the community is dynamic, providing an arena in which teacher-researchers feel confident to share their experiences and findings but also one in which they can expect to be asked tough questions. In this way, the quality of research and the learning of individuals and communities of practice are promoted.

Diversity in action research

In the model in Figure 1.3 we have put intention at the top and this reflects our belief that the enquiry, the burning question, the personal interest, is the key to the development of the research engaged professional. Engaging in enquiry requires teachers to access strategic and reflective thinking, considering the meaning of their activity in holistic as well as analytic ways:

> This kind of thinking is important when embarking on activities which make considerable demands on a person, such as an academic or vocational course or project. It can also be extremely valuable in dealing with … a challenge to an assumption, belief or a communication problem. Most significantly, it is what changes what could be a routine process into a learning experience. (Moseley, Baumfield et al. 2005: 315)

It is by focusing on the intention of the action research that the impetus of the enquiry and the agency of the teacher are made explicit, and strategic and reflective thinking can be most readily accessed. This is not, however, the only orientation for action research and Figures 1.4, 1.5 and 1.6 represent other possibilities.

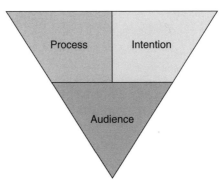

Figure 1.4

In Figure 1.4 intention and process are privileged over the demand to address an audience beyond the teacher or teachers involved. This version of action research is sometimes described as therapeutic. The aim is to engage in a process of self-transformation through the process of enquiry and whilst this may be made public, the main intention is to change the individual and, impact on their practice.

Figure 1.5 illustrates how the trend in policy-driven initiatives to promote evidence-informed practice has tended to privilege the orientation of activity towards the audience for the outcomes rather than focusing on the process or the intention dimension. The main intention here is the sharing of good, or best, practice and the engagement of teachers, policy makers and researchers in dialogue and the exchange of ideas. In some representations of this view, the teachers' enquiry is a precursor to a more considered engagement with existing research; engaging in research in order to engage with research.

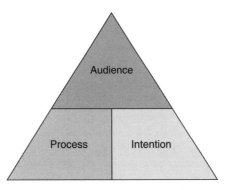

Figure 1.5

Action research located within more traditional academic contexts tends to orient the process away from explicitness on the intentions of the activity towards concentrating on the process and the audience (see Figure 1.6). Whilst the

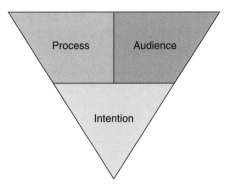

Figure 1.6

intentions are important the value of the activity is seen as being located in the integrity of the processes involved and the aim is to create public knowledge and so audience is a prime concern.

It is important to emphasise that the model of the dynamics of the action research cycle recognises that all three components are present within the different orientations and it is not a matter of judging one against the other but simply being aware that different criteria, different warrants for action, are afforded by the different configurations. Whilst it may be possible to locate particular projects within one of these orientations, they would also incorporate aspects found within other approaches. Problems arise with judgements made from a perspective that privileges one particular orientation and finds any other approach to be deficient rather than different. The standards used to judge the outcomes of research are by no means unproblematic and this is one of the main anxieties of teachers new to research. There are key elements – clarity of reporting, appropriate application of methods selected, ethical considerations – which would be expected in any research project. In our model, the rigour of an individual project is determined by the extent to which the particular orientation is made explicit and subsequently, how well the different aspects are integrated.

Partnerships

Underlying our approach is the principle of '*systematic enquiry made public*' (Stenhouse, 1981). The teachers whose case studies inform this book identified questions and initiated changes in their classrooms that were of interest to them and designed an enquiry that was meaningful in their context. The intended audience for this enquiry was characterised as a 'sceptical colleague' who needs to be convinced of the value of the investigation and its outcomes. The enquiries were usually conducted by pairs of teachers within a school and situated within a supportive network of teachers and university researchers, who operated as co-learners:

crucially, the results of the enquiry have to be related meaningfully both within and beyond their immediate context.

Teacher enquiry has been criticised for the difficulties of generalising results from projects beyond their specific context. Whilst it has high validity for the teacher and the school within which the research was completed, its reliability and transferability can be questioned. This means that the role of partnerships in supporting the teacher-researchers can be crucial. The collaborative nature of enquiry into teaching and learning, which is a feature of many current models of action research in schools, is important, as this helps teachers to develop a professional discourse about learning and provides opportunities for the sharing of ideas across different institutional contexts. Collaboration is a significant aspect of professional development in schools (Cordingley et al., 2005) and this book represents the outcomes from partnerships with schools in a range of different contexts and over a number of years in which the crossing of boundaries has stimulated reflection and enquiry into the processes of teaching and learning in classrooms (Baumfield and Butterworth, 2007).

Structuring this book

In this chapter we have discussed what we believe to be the importance of teacher enquiry through a process of action research for developing and innovating teaching and learning practice. We have outlined a typology exploring the different elements of action research and how they can be configured in different approaches to enquiry. This book will now go on to look at the practical issues of engaging in research into your own practice from the initial identification of a focus to the sharing of your enquiry with a wider audience.

In Chapter 2 we will exemplify the process of refining the focus of the enquiry, choosing an initial research question, checking it is sensible and manageable and then matching data collection tools to answer it. This chapter will go through the process of focusing your research question to limit impacting variables and making sure that the question is a realistic one which can be answered within the context of the teachers' realm. This is where we make the case for multiple approaches using PMIs (Plus–Minus–Interesting points) for the main groups of research methods and then explore diagrammatically and with exemplification in real world case studies how one can overcome weaknesses of one by pairing with another, or how, if methods with corresponding weaknesses are chosen, this must be reported and acknowledged. This multi-method approach will suggest that both quantitative and qualitative methods are appropriate as well as process and outcome related data collection tools.

Chapters 3–5 will, in turn, explore collecting data from pupils, teachers and from parents and the wider community. Each chapter will examine different data collection methods which can be used appropriately for each of these groups. The advantages and disadvantages relating to the different types of evidence will be discussed and some of the ethical issues highlighted. We will focus on data that is already routinely collected in the school and how this can be practically supplemented. Within this, we will focus on a range of examples of research questions, including attainment focused and socio-cultural (talk) and how schools have approached them, both in terms of how tools are used and how they are analysed. These will be linked back to the typology, to show how various approaches place different demands on teachers and yield different results.

Chapter 6 is about interpretation rather than analysis and returns to the issue of weighting various kinds of evidence, clarity about what does and does not constitute an answer to a research question and the iterative process of question generation, which is the heart of an action research cycle. This chapter includes a discussion of rigour and validity in the context of teacher enquiry.

Chapter 7 looks at the process of making the enquiry public and discusses forms of dissemination and the importance of opening the work to challenge so that learning can continue within and across different contexts.

Key perspectives on enquiry and action research

There is a huge literature exploring enquiry and action research, so the references that follow are intended to be a useful starting point for readers to engage with the debates and the range of views from different traditions.

Dadds, M. (1995) *Passionate Enquiry and School Development: A Story About Action Research*. London: Falmer.

Hammersley, M. (2004) 'Action research: a contradiction in terms?', *Oxford Review of Education*, 30(2): 165–181.

Hopkins, D. (2002) *A Teacher's Guide to Classroom Research*, 3rd edn. Buckingham: Open University Press.

Kemmis, S. and R. McTaggart (1988) *The Action Research Planner*, 3rd edn. Geelong: Deakin University.

McNamara, O. (ed.) (2002) *Becoming an Evidence-based Practitioner*. London: RoutledgeFalmer.

Somekh, B. (2003) 'Theory and passion in action research', *Educational Action Research: Special Issue in Celebration of John Elliott's Contribution to Action Research*, 11(2): 247–64.

Whitehead, J. and McNiff, J. (2006) *Action Research Living Theory*. London: Sage.

References used in this chapter

Baumfield, V. M. and Butterworth, A. M. (2007) 'Creating and translating knowledge about teaching and learning in collaborative school/university research partnerships', *Teachers and Teaching: Theory and Practice*, 13(4). pp. 411–27.

Cordingley, P., Bell, M., Evans, D. and Firth, A. (2005) 'The Impact of Collaborative CPD on Classroom Teaching and Learning', Review: What do teacher impact data tell us about collaborative CPD?' In *Research Evidence in Education Library*. London: EPPI-Centre, Social Science Research Unit, Institute of Education, University of London.

Hammersley, M. (2005) 'The myth of research based practice: the critical case of educational enquiry', *International Journal of Social Research Methodology*, 8(4): 317–30.

Hargreaves, D. H. (1999) 'The knowledge-creating school', *British Journal of Educational Studies*, 47(2): 122–44.

Hattie, J. (2003) *Teachers Make a Difference: What is the Research Evidence? Distinguishing Expert Teachers from Novice and Experienced Teachers*. Sydney: Australian Council for Educational Research.

Huberman, M. (2001) 'Networks that alter teaching: conceptualisations, exchanges and experiments', J. Soler, A. Craft, and H. Burgess, in *Teacher Development – Exploring Our Own Practice*. (eds) London: Paul Chapman. pp. 141–59.

Kemmis, S. and R. McTaggart (1988) *The Action Research Planner*. Geelong: Deakin University.

Moseley, D., Baumfield, V. M., Elliott, J., Higgins, S., Miller, J., Newton, D. and Gregson, M. (2005) *Frameworks for Thinking*. Cambridge: Cambridge University Press.

Stenhouse, L. (1981) 'What counts as research?', *British Journal of Educational Studies*, 29(2): 103–14.

Training and Development Agency (2006) *Draft Revised Standards for Classroom Teachers*. London: Training and Development Agency.

2

Deciding on a Research(able) Question and Choosing Complementary Research Tools

CHAPTER CONTENTS

- Choosing a research question and focusing it to limit the number of variables that impact on it
- Ensuring that the question is answerable within your context and manageable given your other teaching commitments
- Considering what will convince your target audience and potentially sceptical colleagues
- Matching data collection tools to your question and thinking about the advantages and disadvantages of different research approaches
- Balancing your commitments and making the research as meaningful as possible by finding overlaps between teaching and learning objectives in the classroom and your research.

Introduction

Once convinced of the benefit of enquiry and the action research cycle for learning about the teaching and learning process in your context, the next stage is to focus on which aspect you want to explore, what questions you want to ask, what change you are expecting and how you are going to measure/observe that change. This chapter will go through the planning process which should underpin any enquiry, however large or small.

The first stage is to look at the list of questions in Box 2.1, which have been adapted from Martin Denscombe's book, *The Good Research Guide*. This is a useful checklist to frame thinking before and during an enquiry. By the end of this chapter we hope to have talked through all of these aspects and guided you through the process of being able to say 'yes' to all of them.

Box 2.1

Before starting your research you need to make sure that you can answer 'yes' to all of these questions.

1   Does the research project address a concrete issue or practical problem?

2   Is there participation by the practitioner at all stages of the research project?

3   Have the grounds for the partnership between practitioner and any outside expert been explicitly negotiated and agreed?

4   Is the research part of a continuous cycle of development (rather than a one-off project)?

5   Is there a clear view of how the research findings will feed back directly into practice?

6   Has insider knowledge been acknowledged as having disadvantages as well as advantages for the research?

7   Is the research sufficiently small scale to be combined with a routine workload?

8   Have ethical matters been taken into consideration?

Adapted from The Good Research Guide *(Denscombe, 2003).*

This chapter exemplifies the process of choosing a research question, supports the process of checking whether this question is manageable and answerable and then explores how you go about matching data collection tools to answer it. It will go through the process of focusing your research question to limit impacting variables and making sure that the question is a realistic one which can be answered within the teachers' context. We will make the case for multiple approaches for answering the question and for increasing confidence in the 'correct' answer. We will also look at how research tools can also directly support teaching and learning, while also looking at how teaching tools can be used to collect data. We will outline the main groups of research methods and then explore diagrammatically and with exemplification in actual case studies how you can overcome weaknesses of one by pairing it with another, or how, if methods with corresponding weaknesses are chosen, this must be reported and acknowledged. This multi-method approach will suggest that both quantitative and qualitative methods are appropriate as well as process and outcome related data collection tools.

Choosing your research questions

For an enquiry to be fruitful it is important that the area of research is closely related to your own experience as a teacher. It needs to be owned by the teachers who are completing the work and it needs to be located within their own domain as teachers. In our experience, unproductive research tends to be focused away from the practice and context of the teacher-researcher and this means that the teacher does not feel motivated and involved sufficiently to see the research to its conclusion. Successful research also tends to involve 'action'. In other words, there needs to be some kind of translation or development of knowledge and understanding for the teacher for the research to feel effective. This could be a confirmed change in practice or a change in the learning environment, but most likely it will be further questions and hunches to be explored.

When starting out on an enquiry a teacher will have an idea about what they would like to explore and this should be something arising from their own teaching and learning experience and practice. In other words, we suspect that there will be something within the context of the classroom in which you work which you would like to explore further. Formulating a research question might start with considering some of the phrases in Box 2.2. All are excellent starting points for thinking about an enquiry and it is important to recognise that most research has its origins in just such professional musings.

Box 2.2

Starting points for enquiry

- I would like to improve …
- I want to change … because
- I am perplexed by …
- Some people are unhappy about …
- I'm really curious about …
- I want to learn more about …
- An idea I would like to try out in my class is …
- I think … would really make a difference to …
- Something I would like to do is to change …
- I'm particularly interested in …

Once you have conceived an idea or hunch which you would like to base your enquiry around, then you need to start framing your thoughts into a question. Now this can appear easier than it is, because the important aspect of this question is that it is answerable; that is, answerable in terms of the data that it is possible to collect, the measurability of the outcomes and the data collection tools available and practical for use.

The first stage is defining the elements which might change as a result of implementing the change/innovation that you are interested in. So for example, if you think that an approach such as Mind Mapping will support the pupils in their learning, you need to think about how this will be manifested. By improved learning, do you mean better understanding or higher attainment? Or will it be shown in better Mind Maps and what characterises a 'better' Mind Map? You need to ask yourself what you think will change as a direct result of implementing the Mind Map technique.

The second stage is to think about what this change will be and what it will look like. So if we continue with the Mind Map example, if you believe that using this approach will lead to better understanding from the pupils, you need to think about what will be the observable change that you expect to indicate this innovation has had an effect. Will it be the pupils displaying better curriculum knowledge in tasks? Will it be better marks in their coursework? Or will it be longer and more elaborate answers to questions during teacher–pupil or pupil–pupil discussion? In this way the focus of your research becomes more specific and therefore more answerable.

Box 2.3			
Examples of hunches moving to questions			
Hunch	Change	Measure	Question
I'm interested in whether boys' writing will improve after peer assessment	Boys' attainment in writing	Through teacher assessment of writing samples taken through the school year	Will boys' attainment in writing (as assessed using teacher assessments) improve after using peer assessment?
I am thinking about using increased visual cues with pupils on the Autistic Spectrum	Improved behaviour from target pupils in whole class sessions	Use existing behaviour monitoring sheets as stipulated in Individual Education Plans	Does the use of visual cues support the improvement of behaviour for pupils with ASD disorders in whole class sessions?
I want to change the questions that I use in class as I feel that I am not meeting the needs of all pupils	Increased alertness and motivation in class discussions	Observations of on-task/ off-task behaviours	Will using more open questions in class discussions improve the on-task behaviour of all pupils?

As you are becoming clearer as to the focus of your research question the last element to consider is how the type of change that you are expecting can be measured or observed. So again using the Mind Map example, if you have decided to focus on how Mind Maps will support pupils in displaying better curriculum knowledge, then the observable outcomes of this might be to see whether this was the case in pupils' work samples, or it might be higher attainment in factual recall tests.

Box 2.3 gives some examples of hunches that have moved to questions and gives some idea as to the thinking behind the potential change which might occur and how the teacher thought it might be measured or observed. It will probably be apparent by now that there will not be one single solution to any of these issues and questions, but throughout this reflective process you will be continually slimming down your focus. In this way you can begin to ensure that your question is answerable. The next stage is to consider whether the question that you proposed is manageable.

Checking the manageability of the research process

There are two aspects to checking whether your proposed research and the way in which you intend to answer the research questions are manageable and realistic. Firstly, is your question really answerable within the complexities of the classroom context? Secondly, does what you are proposing fit into your workload and into your teaching week or year? This section will broach both these aspects and will ask that, as you plan your research project, you constantly ask whether your research is realistic and whether it is practicable.

The contexts in which we need to undertake research in education, however large or small, from nationwide evaluations to the examination of one to one exchanges, are complex and impacted upon by a huge variety of variables. It is almost impossible to cut out and eliminate all of these variables without putting the teacher and their class in a laboratory – which we do not want to do.

A visual representation of the problem can be seen in Figure 2.1. As a researcher you want to be confident that you are getting the right answer to your question and that there are the minimum number of possible influences which could affect this answer. In other words, you want to be sure that your research design is making as close a link between the input (your innovation/change) and the output (the identified change) as possible, with as little interference as possible from associated and impacting variables on the way.

For example, let us look at the first teacher's question from the previous table, peer assessment (see Box 2.3). For this teacher if peer assessment was the input (see Figure 2.2) then they needed to be sure that they were measuring an appropriate outcome but also, probably as importantly, they needed to know that there were a minimum number of other variables which could impact on this measure. So for

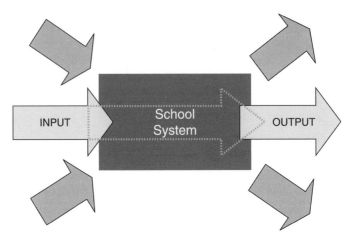

Figure 2.1   The complexity of the school context

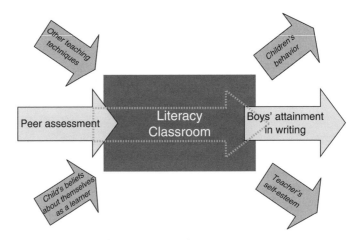

Figure 2.2   The complexity of the literacy classroom

example, they should concentrate on minimising the number of other teaching approaches used to teach writing to this group of boys above and beyond normal practice, and they should consider the attitude of the target group of boys to learning in literacy and, although this is very difficult to control for, try to take it into account.

The other aspect within Figure 2.1 is the outputs. As a researcher you need to examine whether the output which you have focused on, the predicted change or affect of the innovation, is the most appropriate one and the one that is most appropriate as an output of the input. We accept that this output could have been chosen for all sorts of political or personal reasons, whether based on your personal beliefs and your original hunch; whether it is based upon priorities identified at a school level, for example in the School Development Plan; or whether it relates to the need to target a specific group of pupils. Whatever the case, you

Table 2.1   Research Questions and Potential Outputs

Question	Output 1	Output 2	Output 3
Will boys' attainment in writing (as assessed using teacher assessments) improve after using peer assessment?	Boys writing: 1 work samples marked by teacher 2 pupils' self assessments 3 SATs results	Whole classes' writing: 1 teacher assessments 2 SATs results	Teacher confidence: 1 self-critique through use of a learning log 2 interview
Does the use of visual cues support the improvement of behaviour for pupils with ASD disorders in whole class sessions?	Behaviour of pupils with ASD: 1 behaviour log 2 observations 3 video	Achievement of pupils with ASD: 1 Work samples 2 achievement log 3 parental interview	Parental attitudes: 1 questionnaire 2 parenting log
Will using more open questions in class discussions improve the on-task behaviour of all pupils?	On-task behaviour: 1 observations 2 class rewards system 3 pupil self-assessment	Length of pupil contributions: 1 observations 2 video	Pupils' work ethic: 1 SATs results 2 teacher assessment 3 homework return rates

must be able to convincingly answer your research question and therefore you need to check that you are making the most appropriate links and that you are going to be able to collect the evidence to say convincingly that this innovation is having this impact.

Of course, your research might have a more exploratory element to it. In other words you might have a number of ideas of what might be the output but you are not certain. Indeed, even where you might have a recognised output as suggested in your question, you might think, probably quite correctly, that there may be other effects as well. It should always be recognised that with any input into the system there is the potential to change lots of elements within the classroom dynamic. One solution to this dilemma is to collect lots of different data to capture as much information as possible. This is called multi–methods and is discussed later in the chapter. It is enough to say at this point that, even where you are quite convinced of the output, always look for other impacts using the same or different methods. This can be seen in Table 2.1, which uses the example research questions from above, but looks at the potential outputs and how they could be measured.

Table 2.2 **Project Planning Tool**

When	Project tasks	Other school commitments
Term 1 Sept–Oct		
Nov–Dec		
Christmas		
Term 2 Jan–Feb		
Mar–April		
Easter		
Term 3 April–May		
June–July		

One of the disadvantages of collecting more than one type of evidence is that while trying to give the process more clarity and making the associations between inputs and outputs more convincing, then the manageability of the actual process may be reduced.

This 'out of control' feeling can particularly be the case if you do not take time to reconcile the research tasks that you are giving yourself with your workload as a teacher. This is therefore the next element which is essential to making sure that your research is manageable. From our experience this is not a difficult process but means that you need to plan out your research tasks alongside school commitments on a chart, such as the one in Table 2.2. This chart is for the school year; your research might be over a period of time shorter or longer than this – you just need to adapt the timescale to fit.

This chart aims to allow you to plan out your research and make sure that it fits with the school year. So for example, if you are a primary teacher whose class is involved in the school nativity play every year, then to do any data collection in the run up to Christmas might not be appropriate: firstly, the children will be high as kites and therefore any data collected might not be representative, and secondly, if you are involved in rehearsals then your time is going to be pressured and any research is likely to suffer. The same type of thinking might surround a secondary teacher during exam time (both mock and actual), when pupils might be difficult to catch as they are on study leave and there is disruption to the timetable which can leave very little spare time. These types of events, however, can be planned around as they tend to be at fixed or predictable times and the research therefore can be timetabled accordingly.

This process of consideration should support you in being confident that the question is manageable and that it is answerable. This is a necessary balancing act between the evidence which can be collected and the pressures of a teacher's daily/annual routine. The two need to be reconciled as much as possible.

Convincing a sceptical colleague

Once you have thought about manageability, then it is important to think about who you want to convince with your evidence. In other words, who will be your potential audience for your study? This could be colleagues within your school, the senior management team, peers at Local Authority (LA) level or a wider community of enquirers. You will need to decide and think about this as you frame your research design and think about the evidence that it's best to collect to convince your chosen audience.

In addition to choosing the potential audience, we have then found it helpful in research projects to have teachers think of the most potentially sceptical individual in that group and to use them as the target for at least a couple of the evidence sources. We believe it is possible to identify such an individual in most groups and if not then a fictional individual with these characteristics might be appropriate. The quote below from a teacher involved in action research exemplifies this process:

> Action research has proved a very useful tool for supporting the implementation of new ideas and practices in our school. When we were first presented with the idea of action research both my partner researcher and I were interested in its power to persuade reluctant colleagues to have a go at new ideas.
>
> We felt that if we had some kind of proof about the power of the techniques we were employing with the children, other staff would be more motivated to have a go at it themselves. We were right. The fact that our first year of research did not provide us with much quantitative evidence proved unimportant with the rest of the staff. They were most excited, as we had been, by the qualitative findings from the pupil views templates. They were so excited about what children had to say about their learning and the vast difference between the views of the 'Paired Learning' and the control class, that ten out of the fifteen classes wanted to trial it for themselves. (Primary School)

There are so many different data types which you can think about collecting that it is important to sift through which are the most appropriate to your own interests, to your context and to your intended audience. Over the next couple of sections we will outline the different types of evidence which you might think about collecting. As you read through these different ideas it could get overwhelming. We have a broad view of what data can be collected as evidence and, in addition, we will suggest a range of individuals who could be consulted about the impact of change. Therefore, we propose that, while keeping in mind the manageability aspect, you always keep in mind the evidence you would use to convince this sceptical colleague.

Different types of data

In social sciences there are two main types of data which are collected. These are:

- **Qualitative data:** tends to be word based, for example, transcribed interviews
- **Quantitative data:** tends to be number based, for example, test scores.

In social science research there can be a tendency for a researcher to ally themselves with one or the other of these types. So, for example, some researchers might say they are more convinced by quantitative data which means that statistical significance can be looked for; whereas others might argue that this type of number-based data does not give the detail that rich qualitative description and explanation can give. As a broad rule, we tend to see quantitative data as telling you *what* happened on a specific occasion and qualitative data exploring *why* that might have occurred. Examples of each type of data which could be used to explore impact on learners can be seen in Table 2.3.

Table 2.3 Comparing Quantitative and Qualitative Data

	Quantitative	Qualitative
Learners' attainment	Test scores	Interviews
	Teachers' marks	Logs/diaries
	Examples of work	Examples of work
Learners' attitudes	Questionnaire	Interviews
	Survey	Logs/diaries
	Observation/video	Observation/video

There is an added complexity within this division of data and that is because many researchers align the type of data that they collect with their philosophical beliefs about how the world works. This book is not the place to go into this aspect in too much depth, but it is enough to say that researchers that tend towards more quantitative data are likely to say that they are more positivist (objective) in the way that they conceive research design. In other words, a quantitative researcher is more likely to take a scientific approach to their research, with hypotheses to prove/disprove and a predisposition towards experimental and control comparisons. In comparison, a qualitative researcher is more likely to ascribe to an interpretivist (contructivist) standpoint. Thus, they are more likely to accept the complexities of real life research and to adapt their research methods around the variables already in place within a context. Table 2.4 (adapted from Bryman, 2001: 20) exemplifies these philosophical standpoints.

Table 2.4   Comparing Quantitative and Qualitative Approaches

	Quantitative	Qualitative
Principal orientation to the role of theory in relation to research	Deductive; Testing of theory	Inductive; Testing of theory
Theory of how we know	Natural science model; in particular positivism	Interpretivism
Status of knowledge	Objectivism	Constructivism

These are complexities to which some researchers dedicate their whole lives to thinking about; however, the real world teacher-researcher examples below should move these arguments into the classroom context. The first, from Aylward High School, represents a quantitative research method by secondary school science teachers with a positivist outlook. The second is a more qualitative approach from Lanner Primary School and represents the more inductive nature of their enquiry into e-learning logs. As you read through it is possible to see advantages and disadvantages of both approaches. However, at the time when the research was completed, these schools saw these approaches as the most sensible, practical and manageable for them, while also meeting the need to convince their target audience.

Up to this point, we might have made it sound like there is a dichotomy in the potential data that can be collected, but rather we would encourage you to think of it as a flexible relationship between the two elements. Yes, there are researchers who would subscribe to one view or another, but there are others who take a more eclectic approach to their research design, trying to mix and match the best of both worlds. We would argue that you need to think of your audience and apply these types of data accordingly. For example, if your intended audience is policy makers at LA level then you might prioritise SATs or GCSE results and attendance figures as a likely prime concern of these individuals. Whereas, if your audience is other teachers then test scores might be important, but they could also be interested in the attitudes of the learners and the impact on classroom behaviour that the change brought. In other words, in a very pragmatic way such a study might tend to want to explore whether there was a rise in attainment, but also to check whether there was any impact on classroom ethos and atmosphere. In such an example, a method which includes both quantitative (what happened) and qualitative (why it occurred) might be more appropriate. This could be argued to be more meaningful, since as teachers, we want to know about the 'what *and* why' because we are always striving to move forwards in our practice.

Exploring How CASE and Learning to Learn can be Incorporated into Key Stage 3 Science

Stella Onwuemene

Aylward High School, Enfield

Hypothesis

Our hypothesis was that incorporating CASE lessons throughout KS3 Schemes of Work would impact on learning to remember and reflect effectively in different ways thus creating better learners across science KS3–KS4.

Research process

This project focused on the difference between attainment outcomes achieved by each of the three focus classes over the year. Therefore data collected was dominated by attainment scores for a variety of different tests. These included CAT scores and end of topic assessment levels.

Results

From their CAT scores, the classes appear to be equivalent (see graph below). A one way ANOVA also revealed no significant differences between the classes in terms of original CAT scores.

After a year of teaching, the three classes were compared through their members' end of year levels, produced by a SAT type test, and the students' mean levels across three tests. Regressions were also carried out to predict both these outcomes from the CAT scores and the resulting standardised

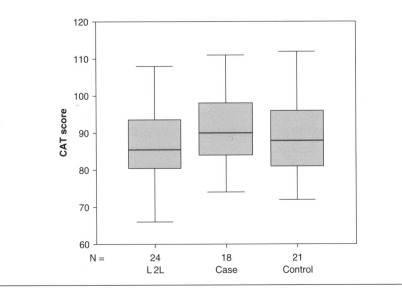

residuals were examined, as measures of gain over the year. The table below shows descriptive statistics for these variables.

A one way ANOVA found no statistically significant differences between most of these means. However, the means of the second standardised residual (the end of year level gain from the CAT scores) do vary significantly ($F = 3.298$, $p = 0.045$) across the classes. The box plots below show the distributions of this standardised residual in the three classes.

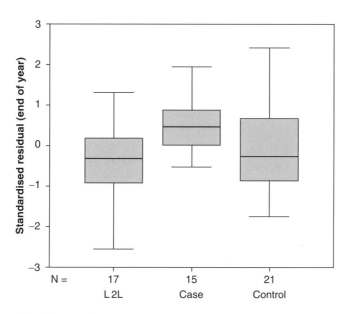

Although the finding of no differences across the other measures of performance should suggest caution, these results do imply that the CASE intervention might improve performance, over either a L2L intervention or no particular intervention. From the box plots, it would seem that the CASE approach might raise the mean performance, but also reduce variation and the tendency for a low-performing tail end of students.

Will Involving Pupils in Reflecting on Learning Through the Use of E-Learning Logs Increase Motivation and Resilience?

Pippa Penda and Liz Martin

Lanner Primary School, Cornwall

Hypothesis

The question we wanted to answer with this research was: will involving pupils in reflecting on their learning increase motivation and resilience?

Research process

Evidence was collected from two main sources:

- Children's reflections in their e-learning logs
- Teacher's observations.

Results

One aspect of reflection to help learning that came from this project was being able to refer to past learning. Some children managed to use the logs to aid SATs revision by looking back on what they had previously learnt. Work on shape in maths and key words in science were used in this way.

It became obvious that the pupils found it difficult to articulate their learning as opposed to what they had done. To help this process a series of questions relating to a reflective journal were displayed in the classroom.

Developing the concepts behind these questions was difficult for most children, even the most able. It was clear that they needed to be introduced earlier, discussed and revisited frequently to make a difference. Probably many of the ideas were too sophisticated to rush through with ten and eleven year olds. In the future the teacher would introduce a few at a time alongside the technology. The whole school approach to assessment for

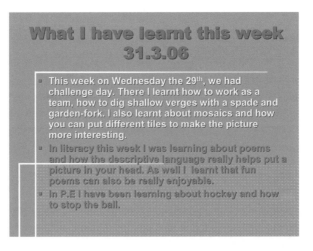

learning will also mean that children are developing the language and concepts as they progress through school.

The initial intention to use the logs regularly through the year did not develop as much as the teacher expected. Sad to say, end of Key Stage 2 test preparation got in the way in the summer term. After the tests we recognise (in hindsight) that many opportunities to continue with the logs were missed. Valuable learning experiences of outdoor education, new school visits and school production were missed.

> However, the pupils' responses showed that they were beginning to recognise the value of the logs in their learning:
>
> 'I like looking back at my slides to remember what we did.'
> 'I had forgotten about converting fractions to decimals but then I saw them in my log.'
> 'The laptops help me add in other things and it looks colourful.'
> 'If I hadn't put the photo in my log I wouldn't have remembered the An Gof tapestry and how good I felt we had done.'
> 'We did dance with Redruth school and worked together really well as a group.'

What constitutes data?

In the previous section, we broached the different types of evidence which are considered by researchers in universities and research institutions outside of schools and we have given some examples as to how this data might be collected in schools. But now we need to consider the role of the teacher–researcher and how this might provide additional insight to different data types, as well as access to evidence which might not be considered, or may not even be available to, researchers from outside of the school. In addition, we are going to argue that these sources of evidence can support the manageability aspect of balancing your research and teaching and learning commitments.

To a broad degree we would define data as widely as possible. In other words, as long as you are answering your research questions and the evidence is meaningful in doing this, then most sources can be construed as research data. Therefore, we would encourage you to be as inventive and as expansive as possible in considering what data collection tools you are going to use in your own research. The following categories of potential data should be useful in this thinking:

- **Traditional research methods**   This category includes interviews, questionnaires and observations; all of which are extremely useful in both a quantitative or qualitative research strategy. However, you might like to think about how they can be adapted and used so that they fit with the agendas behind some of the categories below.
- **Data collected normally in schools**   Schools are data rich environments: data is being collected at individual pupil/teacher level, at class level and at school level all the time. For example Individual Education Plan (IEP) records, attendance, behaviour logs and test scores. This type of data does not add much to your workload to collect and has the advantage of often large and consistent data sets across the school.
- **Data arising from teaching and learning activities**   Teachers are always asking different individuals, especially pupils, to do different activities. This category, therefore, asks whether these outputs can be used as part of your research, for example, work samples and learning logs can be used to tell

the story of a child or a group of children's learning over the period of a term or school year. Yes, these are being collected specifically for the research, but they are adding a new element to your practice relating to learning and teaching.

- **Data collection that can be incorporated into school routine**   In that accountability and self-evaluation are current themes within education, then there are various techniques which can be built into this framework and can be part of your research while also fulfilling other elements of a teacher's job. For example, peer observations can be focused around research-based observation schedules and the pupils' school council can be used to survey opinion of the student body.

One of the key practical messages that we want to get across here is that ideally evidence should be collected, where possible, to fulfil more than one purpose. This helps with the manageability of the research process. So, if the register is being taken at the start of a class every session, then this data can be used in your research to explore whether pupil motivation to turn up to your new and improved lessons has manifested in better attendance. If pupils are completing learning logs to aid their reflection on learning across subjects, then ask the students if it is OK for you to look through and identify whether they perceive that they learn more when you use the specific innovation you are interested in. If your research design needs observations to look at teacher behaviours, can you incorporate it into the teaching staff's routine peer observations?

Table 2.5 uses the example research questions which were introduced in the first half of the chapter and explores the types of data which could be collected under these different headings. This is in no way an exhaustive list and there are many other ways in which evidence could be collected and included; indeed the teachers whose questions these were chose different methods again (talked about in the next section). However, the aim is to get you to think not only about the broad range of data which is available to you as a teacher, but also to think about how you can combine the two roles of teacher and researcher to make the process as manageable as possible.

Across our work with teachers we have been amazed at how teachers and schools have gathered research evidence either from existing school routines and structures or have adapted and changed these same routines to fit with the needs of the research. In most cases all agree that this development process of balancing research evidence and traditional teaching and learning evidence has been a positive experience for the teachers involved and for the school as a whole.

Triangulating data: using multi-methods

It might be apparent by now that we are steering you towards collecting more than one type of data to answer your research question; or in research terms, towards using a multi-method approach. This is not meant to be an inevitable decision, but we have a number of reasons which back up our stance. Firstly, we can see the positives and negatives of both qualitative and quantitative approaches.

Table 2.5 Aligning Research Questions with a Range of Methods

Question	Traditional research method	Data collected normally in schools	Data arising from teaching and learning	Data that can be incorporated into school routine
Will boys' attainment in writing (as assessed using teacher assessments) improve after using peer assessment?	Questionnaire to pupils to explore their perceptions of their learning and improvement in writing before and after peer assessment	SATs and complementary teacher assessments collected over the year and then compared to a mean achieved by previous year groups	Work samples from the group of target boys collected on a termly basis to look at the improvement over the year. Both teacher and pupil give comment as to how this improvement manifests	SMT observations of peer-assessment lessons focusing on target pupils and their approaches to writing-based tasks
Does the use of visual cues support the improvement of behaviour for pupils with ASD disorders in whole class sessions?	Interviews with the pupils' teacher and support staff exploring any perceived changes in behaviour and improvements in attention related to the use of cues	Individual pupil observations, an element of each individual pupil's IEP, which look at different behaviours and how often they occur – do lessons where visual cues are used reveal different/improved behaviour?	Using a sorting activity based on a favourite book: can the pupils complete the task better when visual cues are added? Look at the pupil outcomes as well as the teacher perceptions	Incorporating the capture and analysis of video footage of pupils in whole class situations into support assistants' routine for monitoring individual pupil behaviours and for logging in/appropriate behaviours
Will using more open questions in class discussions improve the on-task behaviour of all pupils?	Structured observations of the pupils' contributions and behaviour in lessons where open questions are used and one not (could be based on video footage). Looking at on-task/off-task behaviour and length of utterance from pupils	Logs of negative and positive behaviour, e.g. how many merits achieved or how many sanctions administered, within each lesson. Does it improve when open questioning approaches are in use?	Using a thinking skills activity, e.g. a mystery, investigate whether the pupil–pupil discussion and the outcome is different in a class where open questions are used when compared to when where not. Look for pupil use of open questions	School-wide system of pupil observations exploring what makes a good lesson and what makes pupils engage with the curriculum content and with discussions. Findings fed back to whole school, teaching staff and pupils

Both give valuable insight into answering a research question and therefore we tend to be loath to choose one in preference to the other. As teachers, we believe that it is important to know both what happened (quantitative evidence) as well as why it might have occurred (qualitative evidence).

Secondly, having worked in schools we accept the complexities of the classroom and the way in which it can impact on the research process. There is a need to be pragmatic in matching your research question with the evidence that is available and practical to collect. It is impossible to use all the variables which could impact on the outcome of a change or innovation and, therefore, more than one method aimed at answering a question can increase your confidence that you are matching cause and effect and answering your question. In this section, therefore, we want to exemplify how a multi-method approach can work, how different methods can work together to answer a research question and how collecting data from different perspectives can strengthen your 'case'.

At first, collecting more than one kind of data can seem to be a bit over the top, but when you keep in mind the broad definition of research evidence that was outlined in the previous section then this can become more manageable. So for example, in many of the projects where we have worked with teacher-researchers we have encouraged them to collect at least three different types of data. However, we emphasise that the majority of these data should be either collected anyway in school, should fit in with teaching and learning or fit into existing school structures. In other words, out of three methods we are saying that at the most only one should be anything over and above what is done already. This can be seen in the diagram of an example research project (see Figure 2.3). The research question is answered using three different methods; however, two of them (methods 1 and 3) are not going to impinge on normal practice. Only one of the data collection methods (method 2) is explicitly linked to the research process and therefore will need to be carefully added into the research plan due to time considerations.

So we would say that to make a multi-method approach practicable then mostly use evidence which you have to hand. However, it is useful also to think of the different types of evidence that you are collecting. Returning to the idea that quantitative data can be useful in saying what happened and qualitative data says why, both data types can be seen as useful for putting together the most comprehensive picture of the impact of innovation or change. Therefore, in thinking about the methods that you use it is useful to think across the range of qualitative and quantitative sources. Again in the example above, the teacher has used two qualitative methods (methods 1 and 2) and one quantitative (method 3), and therefore they will hopefully be able to say whether Mind Mapping impacted on homework returns and the marks achieved (exploring *what* the output of the innovation might have been) as well as the perspectives of the pupils and teachers and the Mind Map association with learning objectives (which will hopefully give some insight as to *why* the impact happened).

The final aspect to consider when confirming your choice of methods should be the different perspectives which might be impacted upon by the innovation which you have implemented and how these perspectives might be captured. In

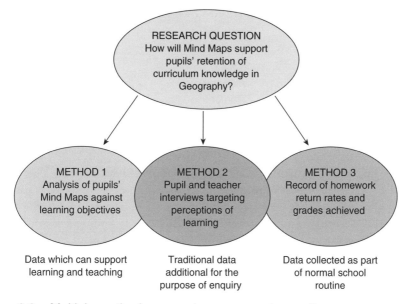

Figure 2.3   Multiple methods answering a research question

Table 2.6, the perspectives of teaching staff and learners are focused on (although it might also be useful to think about parents and the wider school community as well). Here we are starting to think about the internal and external manifestation of the perspectives of these groups.

The external characteristics are more output based. In other words the perspectives of an individual can be observed or recorded. For example, a child who is finding a subject difficult might not behave inappropriately in that lesson; or a teacher who is feeling under-confident with the new ICT equipment they have been given might avoid planning too many lessons using it. In both cases the external characteristics are reflecting the individual's perspective. The disadvantage of relying on this kind of data is that as a researcher you have to interpret the behaviours correctly and without the specific individual's input – it has to be asked – how you can guarantee that your third party interpretation is correct. This is where the internal perspectives become an important counterpoint. Individual and group thinking, beliefs and attitudes about an innovation are really important in exploring perspectives on an innovation. By asking what they believe then you are getting first hand what their perspective might be. However, it should be recognised that these first hand accounts can be tempered and impacted upon by how the individual reacts to your research agenda or you as a person. You need to consider power relationships (particularly when asking children what they think) and personal agenda which might bias the data.

There are, therefore, disadvantages and advantages to both these methods of capturing groups' perspectives, but again thinking about mixed methods and how you can combine different data collection methods you can go some way to compensate and rationalise your research and what you want to get from it. Thinking

Table 2.6   Exploring a Range of Perspectives

	Internal	External
Learners	Thinking	Behaviours
	Beliefs	Performance
	Attitudes	Examples of work
Teaching staff	Thinking	Behaviours
	Beliefs	Performance
	Attitudes	Planning/marking

carefully about the data that is already available, that which can be collected as part of teaching and learning or school routine, is useful in combining with more traditional methods and your research question is essential in making the process practical and by using more than one method increased confidence in the enquiry can be achieved.

The ethics of research in school

It has been established that classrooms are multi-faceted and extremely complex; therefore, the ethical considerations relating to researching it can be equally intricate and subtle. Many of the predicaments that researchers find themselves in come from the 'costs/benefits ratio': finding a balance between thorough investigation and the privacy of their subjects (Cohen and Manion, 1998). This section will explore the ethical considerations that should be intrinsic to any research design, both in conception and administration. Of particular import with most research in schools, of course, will be the ethical considerations surrounding involvement of pupils in the research.

Having recognised the complexities of educational research, the contexts in which the research is set and the promotion of mixed method approaches means that any ethical guidelines have to be the overarching ones under which research occurs. The British Education Research Association (BERA)[1] offers a set of principles and advice which can support the aim of ethical research. Box 2.4 gives an overview of these guidelines.

Box 2.4

The Association [BERA] considers that all education research should be conducted with an ethic of respect for:

- the person
- knowledge
- democratic values
- the quality of education research
- academic freedom.

With regard to teacher-research then the ethical considerations about people are likely to be the most important. You have to think about how you are treating all people, whatever their age, sex and background, directly and indirectly involved in the research. Voluntary informed consent is important and in the case of children it is essential that this is not only obtained from the parents, which as teachers tends to be one of our first considerations, but also from the children themselves. If you are researching children's perspectives or behaviour then you need to inform them as to your research (in accordance with Article 12 and 13 of the United Nations Convention on the Rights of the Child[2]) and also the role that they are going to play within it. If you are asking their opinion then it is important that you do not deceive them, that they know why and how the research will be done and that they are able to drop out if they wish at any stage. This is hard because as a teacher you are likely to be used to being in control; for example, we have often spoken to teachers who are thinking about recording pupil talk without their knowledge. As teachers we do this as we assess progress, but in research particularly when you are intending on making the findings public then you have to consider whether it is appropriate and ethical. To get accurate and ethical results you need to make sure individuals give informed consent and understand what you are enquiring about. These points are important with children, but they should not be forgotten when working with adults as well.

In addition to thinking about consent, you also need to think about whether incentives are appropriate – a good bribe can work a treat with children and grown-up children alike – but you need to use common sense as to the appropriateness of what you are offering and whether they will impact on the outcomes of the research. For example, a prize draw for all completed questionnaires returned by parents will go a long way to improving return rates and it should not impact on the answers given as a draw does not rely on the answers given.

We have previously mentioned that part of the systematic enquiry approach we are suggesting is the making public of any findings. When you do disseminate your findings the privacy of your participants must be assured and they must be reassured of this right from the beginning: you would not want to give your honest opinion of how your school is run if there was a chance that your potentially controversial thoughts might be traced back. It is important that you give participants the right to confidentiality and to anonymity and this should stretch to how you store the data as well as how you report your research.

The final aspect which we believe makes for good ethical research is the closure of the feedback loop. To show that you are genuine about the contributions made by your participants, whether time taken to talk to you, to filling in your questionnaire or to allowing access to teaching and learning, then you need to make a commitment to feeding back your findings back to these participants. With the pupil voice agenda currently prevalent in schools pupils are being asked more and more regularly for their opinions, but very rarely are the findings and indeed the resulting actions taken on their behalf fed back. We believe that this is really important for fulfilling the BERA ethical guidelines.

Matching data collection tools to questions

In this chapter we have asked you to think about your research questions and to make sure that it is answerable and manageable alongside your other teaching commitments. We have suggested that you think about different research approaches and to weigh up the advantages and disadvantages of each with a target audience and potential sceptical colleague in mind. In addition, we have outlined the range of data that can be used in answering your research questions and the extent to which an overlap between your research and teaching and learning objectives in the classroom can be useful in balancing your own commitments as well as making the research as meaningful as possible.

The last thought we would like to leave you with, as you head into the three chapters on collecting data from teachers, pupils and parents and the wider school community, is that, whatever evidence you choose to use and whichever data collection tools you incorporate into your research design, you need to make sure that they link back and answer your research question. You need to make sure that the processes are manageable, that you can rationalise your choice of method and that you can achieve confidence that you have answered your question appropriately.

Key perspectives on research design

Lewis, I. and Munn, P. (1997) *So You Want to Do Research! A Guide for Beginners on How to Formulate Research Questions.* SCRE Publication No. 136. Edinburgh: SCRE.

References used in this chapter

Bryman, A. (2001) *Social Research Methods.* Oxford: Oxford University Press.
Cohen, L. and Manion, L. (1998) *Research Methods in Education*, 4th edn. London: Routledge.
Denscombe, M. (2003) *The Good Research Guide, 2nd edn.* Berkshire: Open University Press.
Leat, D. (1998) *Thinking Through Geography.* Cambridge: Chris Kington Publishers.

Notes

1 http://www.bera.ac.uk/publications/guides.php
2 http://www.unicef.org/crc/

3

Taking Account of Pupil Perspectives in Your Enquiry

CHAPTER CONTENTS

- The values of consulting pupils and their contribution to our understanding of teaching and learning
- Methods for exploring three key areas: observed behaviour; evidence of learning; pupils' thinking and beliefs
- How to make good use of existing data on pupils
- Examples of some data collection tools and case studies showing how they have been used in schools.

Introduction

This chapter presumes that, as many teachers do, you have made a decision to investigate pupils in some way as part of your enquiry. This could be a consultation of attitudes or beliefs or it could be an exploration of pupil behaviours or an investigation of learning outcomes. It could be with regard to school structures, organisation and management or the process of teaching and learning. Regardless of the focus, this chapter will explore the different evidence sources which can be used to do this, the different methods which might be used and the issues and considerations which are important when researching pupil perspectives.

In 1989, Article 12 of the UN Convention on the Rights of the Child increased the emphasis on the entitlement of pupils to have their voice heard regarding situations and contexts which impacted on them. It states that: 'children and young people have a right to be involved in the decisions that affect them. This right extends from decisions affecting them as individuals, to decisions that affect them as a collectivity.' Since this legislation, the rationale for consulting pupils has diversified and the potential significance of the pupils' perspective has been established within the context of education. From a policy perspective, the DfES has commissioned research in the field (for example,

Clark et al., 2003) and Ofsted has developed consultation of pupils as part of inspections (Ofsted, 2003). Within research projects, pupil views of school structures and teaching and learning are becoming increasingly common as a perspective to be seriously considered (for example, Pollard, 1996; Tunstall and Gipps, 1996). In practice, partly facilitated by new inspection criteria, but also through a genuine recognition of the stake that pupils have in a school system, pupils are also increasingly being asked their opinion, for example, through the use of school councils (Osler, 2000; Alderson, 2000) and through 'students as researchers' initiatives (Raymond, 2001; Worrall, 2000). Some of this thinking can be seen in this list of the advantages of pupil consultation adapted from Flutter and Ruddock (2004) (see Box 3.1).

Box 3.1

Advantages of pupil consultation

In their book, *Consulting Pupils: What's in it for Schools?*, Julia Flutter and Jean Ruddock (2004) give a number of reasons why pupil consultation is a key to improving teaching and learning:

For pupils
Involving pupils in the discussion about teaching and learning:

- develops an understanding and awareness of learning processes
- helps pupils to see learning as a serious matter
- promotes the development of higher order thinking skills (metacognition)
- raises pupils' self-confidence and self-esteem
- allows pupils to acquire technical language for talking about learning.

For teachers
Involving pupils in the discussion about teaching and learning:

- offers teachers feedback to help improve aspects of their practice
- can offer help to improve the quality of teacher–pupil relationships
- enables teachers to identify problems impeding pupils' progress
- helps to create a more collaborative classroom environment
- can be used to develop new ideas to improve teaching and learning.

For schools
Involving pupils in the discussion about teaching and learning:

- may suggest new directions for school improvement planning
- can contribute to monitoring and evaluating processes for school self-review
- helps to establish a more positive learning culture within the school

> - provides a practical expression of ideas taught in citizenship education
> - encourages pupils and teachers to feel that they are valued and respected members of an inclusive, collaborative learning community.

There is little doubt that within the work we have done with schools and teachers, that investigation of the pupils' perspective has been both informative and sometimes unexpectedly influential in informing school development and innovation. It is not an unproblematic area of enquiry, but with careful thought and implementation you can reap the rewards.

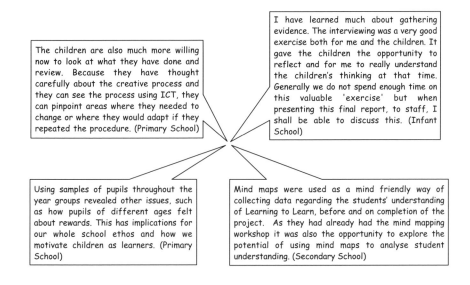

The children are also much more willing now to look at what they have done and review. Because they have thought carefully about the creative process and they can see the process using ICT, they can pinpoint areas where they needed to change or where they would adapt if they repeated the procedure. (Primary School)

I have learned much about gathering evidence. The interviewing was a very good exercise both for me and the children. It gave the children the opportunity to reflect and for me to really understand the children's thinking at that time. Generally we do not spend enough time on this valuable 'exercise' but when presenting this final report, to staff, I shall be able to discuss this. (Infant School)

Using samples of pupils throughout the year groups revealed other issues, such as how pupils of different ages felt about rewards. This has implications for our whole school ethos and how we motivate children as learners. (Primary School)

Mind maps were used as a mind friendly way of collecting data regarding the students' understanding of Learning to Learn, before and on completion of the project. As they had already had the mind mapping workshop it was also the opportunity to explore the potential of using mind maps to analyse student understanding. (Secondary School)

In that there are so many different factors driving the pupil views initiatives, it should be recognised that there can also be differences associated with the way research is undertaken. This includes the contrast between quite formulaic consultation, which could be seen as ticking boxes on school Self-Evaluation Forms (SEF), and more formative processes, which can support school development as well as extending teachers' and pupils' understanding of teaching and learning (Arnot et al., 2004). With reference to these different approaches to collecting data on pupils, there is a real need to think through the reasons why you are asking pupils for their perspective, what you think the outcomes will be and whom they are for. With regard to the theory behind enquiry and the action research cycle proposed in this book, a more formative process would appear to have best fit. But if this is the case then you need to ask to what extent are findings relating to the pupils fed back to them as individuals – do they get a chance to validate (agree/disagree with) the interpretation of their views and do they get a say in the next step of the *action*?

This chapter will be based around the way in which pupil views and perspectives can develop and accentuate feedback loops within the school; the way in which research can be used to encourage communication about learning and teaching between different individuals in school, including the pupils. The authors believe that underlying any true enquiry into the pupils' perspective there must be an authenticity of process. In other words, there needs to be transparency and honesty in the way that the research is rationalised to the pupils and also a commitment to involvement from the pupils at more than a tokenistic level. In addition, it needs to be recognised that there is an outcome, an action, arising from the consultation for it to be meaningful and this also needs to be communicated across participants. Thus, by opening up the rationale to pupils, the action research is not an isolated enquiry by an individual, but becomes an open dialogue about the processes operating in schools and provides an evidenced-based rationale for development and innovation.

We believe that there are three key research areas commonly examined with regard to the pupils' perspective. These are:

1 the observed behaviour (performative data)
2 evidence of learning (data on cognitive outcomes as well as cognitive process)
3 pupils' thinking and beliefs (data on attitude, dispositions and metacognition)

We see these different aspects as overlapping (see Figure 3.1); however, for ease of explanation they will be covered in turn within this chapter and for each section we will look at potential methods for enquiring into these aspects of the pupils' perspective. However, it is always worth remembering the extent to which transfer and overlap can be made, particularly with regard to how one research method can explore more than one of these areas.

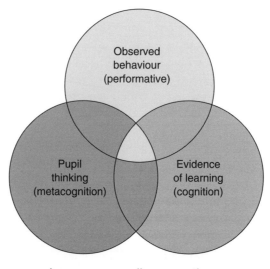

Figure 3.1   Key research areas on pupil perspectives

Within each section we will explore the extent to which evidence is already available, as previously stated schools are data rich environments, and pupil-related data are no exception to this rule: we will ask to what extent can this be taken advantage of and whether this data collection can be extended in any way to make the process more formative and less 'box ticking' (as discussed above). We will also look at data that can be collected in a way that either takes advantage of school structures that are already in place, for example, school councils, or evidence that can support teaching and learning. We will also look at the third aspect which is data that needs to be collected in addition to the previous two, including how pupils can operationalise their own enquiry and become researchers into their own learning.

Observable behaviours (performative data)

Performative data are the observable behaviours which pupils (or indeed any one else) exhibit in reaction to a change in normal practice. For example, a child who does not appreciate a new approach to practical science investigation might decide not to turn up to lessons (data that can be collected through attendance records); or they might express their opinion to the teacher or peers with regard to the changes (data which can be collected through the use of videoed lessons); or they may be observably more often off-task in these lessons than in other lessons (data that can be collected through an on-task/off-task observation schedule). All of these look in some way at the outcome of the change with regard to the pupils.

To research this aspect of pupils, data that is collected from students routinely as part of the day-to-day running of a school and the normal process of the class-room seems to be a fairly reasonable option. For example, work and attainment are assessed regularly, attendance is monitored daily and behaviours observed (from informal classroom management to formal behaviour monitoring). These processes can easily be used as part of an enquiry; indeed, we would positively encourage their use as a source of data as they help to make research practicable and meaningful to the busy teacher.

Having said this, there are various ways in which this crossover between teaching and research can be made more explicit and therefore more manageable. Pupil track-ing is a useful way of collecting and triangulating data that is routinely collected in schools, giving an overview of specific pupils' school experience. The information sheet given in Table 3.1 indicates the type of data which could be collected and how regularly it might be collected. This list is in no way exhaustive and the timings will vary between schools, but as a broad outline it has been shown to be useful.

This type of information can stand alone as research evidence to support teaching and learning, but you need to consider whether this is truly the pupils' perspective or whether it is pupil outcomes only. Both have their value, but to increase the mean-ingfulness of your enquiry it is often better to also ask the pupils about the context surrounding these behaviours and why they might have happened (either a question-naire or an interview). Alternatively, the evidence could be used more directly as the starting point for an interview with a specific pupil or the whole class. In this way

Table 3.1 Information Collection for Pupil Tracking

This sheet is a guide to the kinds of information that could be collected as part of student tracking. For each piece of information there is a suggestion of how often the data should be collected: yearly, monthly, weekly or daily. Obviously, this list is not exhaustive and within your project you will need to use data which relates to your research hypothesis and fits in with school policy and practice. This is just a guide: it is not exhaustive or laid in stone. Where more than one box is shaded, you need to decide which information is collected and how often.

Information type / When to be collected	Yearly	Termly	Monthly	Weekly	Daily
SATS/GCSE/A level results (& other standardised tests)	▓				
Teacher's formative assessment		▓	▓		
Individual Education Plan updates and SEN paperwork		▓	▓		
Work samples			▓	▓	
Behaviour log				▓	▓
Attendance				▓	
Pupil views on their achievement		▓	▓		
Parent views on their child's achievement	▓	▓			
Record of task completion				▓	▓
Observation (in class or, for example, in playground)		▓	▓	▓	
Record of successes			▓	▓	▓

the evidence is presented to the pupils and they are asked to explain why they think it says what it does and to rationalise any oddities in the data or think about how it could be changed. Through using either of these approaches the whole direction of the consultation and involvement of pupils in the enquiry changes. An example of this research rationale can be seen exemplified by the quote below. It was taken from a research project undertaken as part of an MEd dissertation and describes how, as part of an interview, a pupil with ADHD was presented with evidence regarding his behaviour record and his opinion of the correlations made with when he has taken his medication.

When asked about what he knew about ADHD he said, 'I don't really know but I've had it a long time and need to take tablets to help me' (interview 2006).

I asked him what kind of symptoms he has as a result of ADHD and he said when his tablets wear off at home he is 'silly' and 'jump around a lot'. He said that his ADHD makes him behave badly in class 'most of the time' and when I expressed surprise at this, he said this was when he does not take his tablets. According to Peter he is 'always bad at home' and not very 'helpful' and this is the time when he is 'silly' and 'jumps around a lot'. (Secondary School)

If we return to the three-way Venn diagram introduced earlier, then this is where you start to cross over from performative data to pupils' thinking: you are not only recording and analysing the observable behaviours, but you are also exploring the pupil's reasoning as to why they happened.

Another approach to collecting the performative data might be to use video of teaching and learning, for example, footage of the lesson or event about which you are enquiring. Some tips as to the practicalities of using video in the classroom are included in Box 3.2 and these issues should not be underestimated. Using video is a really effective way of collecting the most comprehensive data from a context; however, on the down side, it can create a vast amount of data to be analysed (sometimes an overwhelming amount, particularly for a busy teacher). Nevertheless, there are ways in which it can be made manageable. This could be through limiting the amount of time which is to be included as footage for the research or by limiting analysis specifically to the question which you want to answer. For example, focusing on a specific section of a lesson like plenaries or a specific group working together rather than the whole class for the whole of the lesson automatically concentrates the data for your enquiry; or if the whole lesson is necessary then you can focus the analysis of the footage by being clear about what you are looking for and by limiting the way in which it is used. This could be done by focusing on just the questions asked by the teachers and how they are responded to or by targeting your analysis to the behaviours of a specific sample of children (who can be chosen for a variety of reasons: a representative sample, individual characteristics etc.).

Box 3.2

Top tips for using video in the classroom

- Make sure that there is sufficient tape or space on a disk (if digital video).
- Work out where the electricity points are in the classroom (your cable may not be long enough).

(Continued)

- If using a battery, make sure that there is enough power for the recording you want to do.
- Try not to swoop and zoom too much too quickly as it's difficult to watch later.
- Try to avoid zooming in on children as it can cause a distraction.
- Do an on-the-spot trial and replay to make sure you are recording.
- Make sure that your sound equipment is adequate. It is often difficult to discern individual voices in a classroom environment and this can make the process of transcription even more demanding.
- Think about the purpose of your study and the operation of the camera. If you want to observe whole class interaction in order to develop an hypothesis about your teaching behaviour, for example, then you will have to think about who will operate the camera, and what impact the 'extra body' is likely to have on pupils' reactions. If, on the other hand, you want to observe a group interaction in order to examine a specific pupil or teaching strategy, then you may wish to set the recorder at some distance from the group (i.e. not manually operated). In this case, it is wise to check the level of classroom noise and whether individual voices can be clearly recorded.
- **Make sure** that you have received **parental** and **pupil permission** prior to recording. This is essential given the possibility of religious objections and current policies on child protection issues. Check the school and local council policies prior to sending out a letter requesting permission.
- Make sure all parties concerned agree to later access rights (to the recordings) as this will impact on parental consent (especially for children on an 'at risk' register). This is particularly important if you are thinking of putting any visual images in a publication or on an internet site. Refer to the Becta website for further information: http://schools.becta.org.uk/index.php?section=is

As before with the pupil tracking data, research with video can be made into a more formative process of enquiry by involving the pupils in the process of video capture as well as the analysis. With the former, where pupils have been given the job of taking the video with a specific focus in mind, then an additional level of data analysis can be based upon what the pupils chose to film and their rationale for it:

- Why did you film this?
- Why did you not film that?
- Why do you think it is a good example of this teaching and learning?

The quote below comes from a case study written by a teacher in a nursery school (pupils in the target class ranged in age from three to four and eight months) and shows how video cameras were used to support the pupils in enquiring into their own and their peers' learning, while also supporting the enquiry of the teacher at a meta-level.

> The children were fascinated by the video camera so Mrs H introduced a small hand-held camera for the children to use. This was very exciting for them and they all wanted to try. Obviously, it was not as easy as it looked and the less able children struggled. However, she persevered and a number of children were able to record their friends' activities.
>
> Some children even had the confidence to ask questions as they were recording their friends' activities. The whole group enjoyed watching the 'playback' and it encouraged more children to have a try.
>
> As the children became accustomed to the presence of the camera, they soon forgot about it and some excellent work was recorded. One section of the film which was very useful to show parents was a child 'reading' a 'Percy' book to her friend during milk time. She was able to follow conventions such as giving the title of the book, turning the pages carefully and showing the illustrations. She also repeated the story almost word perfect and showed obvious enjoyment whilst doing so. (Nursery School)

Involving the pupils in the analysis of video can also be useful, particularly to initiate a discussion about learning. Specific sections can be used as prompts or for an interview (for example, *what you were doing here was interesting: can you talk me through what was going on?*) or the pupils can be asked to choose specific bits and talk about what is happening and why (for example, *I am interested in effective group work, can you choose me a video clip which you feel represents this and tell me why you chose it?*). In this way the videoed behaviours are being interpreted by the pupils themselves and, therefore, the meaningfulness of the interpretation and the research itself is increased.

A third option would be an observation schedule in probably its most traditional sense. This research method may need a third person, or some training for pupils if they are to use it, but can provide very specific and consistent information about the behaviours of pupils at different points in a lesson or as a comparison across sessions. A popular observation schedule, which has been used across projects, is the 'on-task/off-task behaviour observation' (see Table 3.2).

This observation schedule is based on a process of time-sampling. It is very difficult for an observer to keep accurate and consistent observations continually for more than 10 minutes and so this is why time-sampling is essential. Time-sampling means that observations are taken for just a percentage of the lesson or environment being observed. The main ways this can be done is through:

- scanning; or
- chunking.

Table 3.2 Systematic Observation of Individual Pupils

SCHOOL:	Observe the pupil every 5 minutes and record their behaviour at the time		BEHAVIOURS	Tally Chart of Observed Behaviours for 5 focus pupils					
				Pupil 1	Pupil 2	Pupil 3	Pupil 4	Pupil 5	TOTAL
CLASS:		ON TASK	Talk related to task						
DATE:			Answering question						
			At work						
LESSON:			Listening to teacher/peer						
TEACHER:		OFF TASK	Talk not task related						
SUBJECT:			Wandering around room						
OBSERVER:			Attempting to draw attention						
			Day dreaming						
			TOTAL						

Scanning means that the whole area is scanned every two, five or ten minutes (the timing is chosen depending on manageability and context) and the behaviours observed at each moment in time are noted down through a tally. A picture is built up over time. This observation schedule allows you to focus on a specific group of pupils (chosen as either representative of the class or because their characteristics fit with the nature of the enquiry) and identify their predominant behaviours over the duration of the lesson. The example below comes from a primary school where the observations were completed by a member of teaching staff to explore behaviours in different learning environments.

Example

Observation of the class indicated that children had become more motivated in their own learning. Over the year they appeared to become less reliant on the teacher to direct their learning and keep them focused and on task. The children began to appear excited when making their choice of activity and looked forward to visiting the different learning environments.

When carrying out formal observations on five separate occasions over the year it was evident that the number of children who remained on task (motivated to learn) for the duration of the self-initiated session (L2L session) had dramatically risen.

During the summer term observation, out of the 15 children observed in the session; all remained on task for 40–45 minutes (the duration of the

	Number of pupils and total time spent on task				
	0–9 mins	10–19 mins	20–29 mins	30–39 mins	40–45 mins
Autumn 2nd	4	2	4	5	0
Spring 2nd	2	2	6	4	1
Spring 2nd	0	3	2	6	4
Summer 2nd	0	0	4	3	8
Summer 2nd	0	0	0	0	15

session), an improvement on the other half terms and a considerable improvement on the autumn 2nd and spring 1st half term.

The same group of children were observed on each separate occasion and it is evident from the findings that there was a 100% per cent increase on the number of pupils who remained on task for the duration of the lesson in the summer 2nd half term compared to the autumn term. It is, however, not possible to conclude if the increased age and maturity of the pupils over the year could have contributed to the findings and, if so, by how much? (Primary School)

As with other pupil perspective methods, this kind of data could be shared with the pupils to gain a further insight into its meaning and to support the analysis. This might be particularly useful if the pupils themselves have been involved with using the schedule and observing each others behaviours.

Evidence of learning (cognition)

Evidence of learning is the main 'business' of schools. As a result, there are many different data collection strategies which build upon information routinely collected as part of teaching and learning. This can include standardised attainment data (for example, GCSE results), teacher assessments, peer assessment and self-assessment of learning. Each has its advantages and disadvantages, often related to the summative or formative nature of different assessment types, and as a researcher you need to approach each from a critical standpoint and make sure that the most appropriate is chosen for answering your research question and for triangulating with other data collected. However, this section is not just about assessment – it can also be about the process of cognition – which is harder to capture, but can be explored through observations of talk in the classroom (this could be, for example, pupil–pupil or teacher–pupil talk).

Standardised assessments are commonly used in research projects. This is often because it is a language that policy makers appear to recognise and pay attention to. It is a common perception that for an innovation to be effective then it needs to raise standards, standards as measured by national tests (SATs, GCSEs, and AS/A Level). It also has to be recognised that this is a popular and commonly understood discourse in schools and associated communities. It is a language (of subjects, curriculum and grades/levels) that is easily recognised and, particularly in secondary schools, is one that tends to dominate much of the talk about teaching and learning. As such this type of data is useful to collect as part of your research and, if there is an improvement in results, can have a tendency to convince more people of an innovation's success. However, it should also be noted that to achieve an improvement in SATs or GCSE results that can be attributed to a single innovation is difficult. There is so much going on in school, so many new innovations: change and development related to school structures, to the curriculum and to pedagogy are endemic at the moment, and so pinpointing which may have actually caused the change is hard and often unrealistic.

An example of action research using GCSE results can be seen below. In this section it is possible to see that the teacher has compared the GCSE results for two groups in the same Year 11: those involved in the mentoring programme and those that were not. There are ethical issues which need to be considered in relation to using a control group like this: to what extent is it ethical to implement an innovation which you as a teacher believe in to one group of pupils and not to others, when these pupils will not have the chance to do their GCSEs again? If, on the other hand, the whole year group are included in an innovation results would need to be compared in an alternative way, for example by comparing with mean data across previous year groups (a mean should account for any year group variation) or by relying on comparing predicted with actual. As before, each has potential consequences, advantages and disadvantages, and so has to be carefully considered before   being put into operation.

Example

Twenty-five students took part in the mentoring programme. These were students whose performance at GCSE was giving cause for concern. They were statistically capable of grade C at GCSE in a number of subjects (five or more) but were, according to teacher assessment data, working below or well below this level in most subjects.

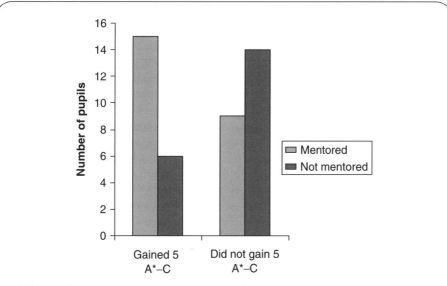

Fifteen of the 25 students gained 5 A*–C grades, a success rate of 60%. Of the 240 separate GCSE examinations taken by this cohort, the results in the top three grades were:

- 3 A grades
- 27 B grades
- 386 C grades

Of the grades gained by this cohort, 48% were A*–C. It should also be noted that had four of the students managed to turn one of their D grades into a C, the success rate for the cohort would have been 76%.

The graph summarises the results for 44 students targeted. It can be seen that 60% of students in the target group who engaged on the programme gained 5A*–C grades, whereas 30% of students in the target group who did not engage on the programme gained 5A*–C grades. (Secondary School)

One way in which, as an action researcher, you can feel more confident with your results as being a true reflection of the learning associated with your chosen innovation is to use other sources of information and triangulate them. In other words come at the evidence of learning from two (or even three) different directions. So this could be a triangulation of national tests with teacher assessments. Or it could be that results are backed up by the pupils' opinions, gathered through interviews or questionnaires, about their own learning and their experience of the test themselves. In this way national tests are incorporated into the overall research design, but do not become overly relied upon.

Data on cognition can be gathered in many other ways. The popularity of formative assessment strategies (based on the work of Black and Wiliam (1998) and Clark (2001)) in schools currently means that there is a developing dimension of peer assessment and self-assessment which can be easily incorporated into action research, while also relating closely to dialogue about teaching and learning in the classroom. As can be seen in the case study from Fallibroome High School, peer assessment data has been cross referenced with pupil opinion about their attitude to learning, in this case through the administration of a questionnaire asking pupils about their learning using formative assessment techniques.

There are many outputs to formative assessment strategies which can become data collection tools. For example this could include:

- skills ladders
- learning logs
- peer assessment records
- records of the pupils' use of three stars and a wish (Claxton, 2004)
- self-assessment using feeling fans recorded through a photograph (see Figure 3.2).

Figure 3.2   A photograph collected as research data showing pupils' assessment of their own understanding at the end of a lesson

All these activities are likely to be part of a teacher's pedagogy, while also, without too much additional effort, become data collection to support an enquiry.

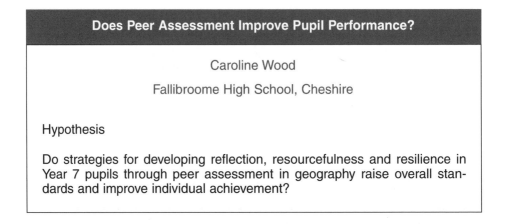

Does Peer Assessment Improve Pupil Performance?

Caroline Wood

Fallibroome High School, Cheshire

Hypothesis

Do strategies for developing reflection, resourcefulness and resilience in Year 7 pupils through peer assessment in geography raise overall standards and improve individual achievement?

Research Process

A number of different evidence sources were used to answer my research questions:

- Mark grids from 7O recording the students' performance both before and after the peer assessment exercise.
- Mark grids from 7E recording the students' performance without experiencing the peer assessment exercise.
- A simple questionnaire survey of 7O, to see how they felt about the peer assessment exercise.
- A video of the peer assessment lesson was recorded.

Results

When comparing the quality of work produced by both classes, the percentage of students within each class achieving a particular position on the mark grid were compared to eliminate the problem of having slightly different sample sizes on the day, due to pupil absences.

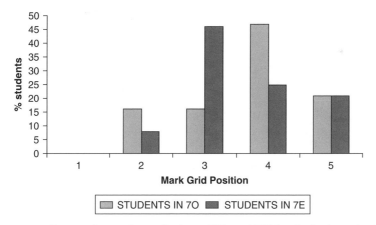

Comparison of results from 7O and 7E for factual content

The results showed that a greater proportion of students achieved the highest grid position in 7O than 7E in three out of the five areas of the mark grid. This is shown in the graph above and below with regard to the skills of mapping and factual content.

Pupils in 7O were invited to comment on a simple questionnaire, regarding whether or not they felt the peer assessment lesson had helped them. All of their responses were positive, including:

'The comments my partner gave me helped me to realise what I needed to improve.'

The general feeling from the students was that they felt that it was easier to use the grid and that they could more confidently assess their peers with a mark grid than if they had been asked to write their own feedback comments. The students who took part in the peer assessment lesson seemed

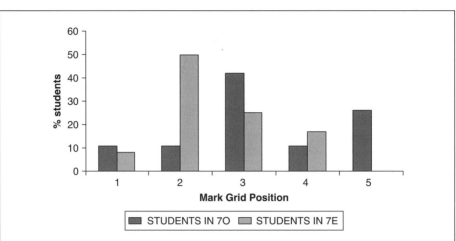

Comparison of results from 7O and 7E for maps and diagrams

to be able to write some meaningful comments on their partners' evaluation sheet. In general discussion with the students, they felt that the scaffold had helped them write their usual evaluative paragraphs but they also felt that there was an overkill on the, 'I particularly liked' – one overall comment would have sufficed.

The most important impact of my findings is that peer assessment exercises such as the one covered in this project will be used on a much more regular basis across all years in geography. The project has been extremely successful in highlighting the benefits of AfL.

All of these data collection strategies rely on some kind of recordable outcome, so what about the cognitive *process*, is there a way of gathering evidence of learning in action? Group work, discussion and dialogue about learning are all important pedagogical strategies and so it is important that evidence of learning does not just become dominated by assessment, whether formative or summative. This type of learning can be evidenced through the incorporation of some kind of output into a task, for example:

- photographs (which could be annotated by the pupils) of the different stages of a practical activity (see example below);
- allocate role of scribe within each group with job of recording discussion;
- tape or video record discussions in class; or
- get pupils to record main points of discussion through a mind map.

Example

The teacher wanted the whole class to be involved in the process and so had to design a strategy which was appropriate and achievable for all 22 children, whilst also being manageable for the teacher.

The children were very confident in saving, retrieving and creating files in many applications and they were also comfortable with downloading pictures and placing them in documents. Even though they had not been taught how to use *PowerPoint* or how to create and add sound files they acquired these skills very quickly and easily.

In groups of three or four the children were asked to design an ancient Greek monster with at least one part to move using pneumatics. They had an afternoon to design, create and evaluate the monsters and after every half an hour a digital photograph of the model was taken and the children were asked to write down where they were in the design process and any adaptations they had been forced to make so far. (Primary School)

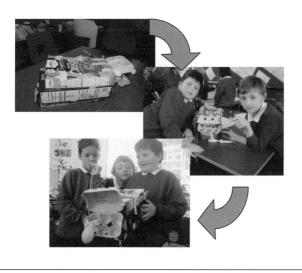

This list is in no way exhaustive, there are all sorts of ways in which this kind of task can be tweaked to provide evidence.

What, however, do you do if you feel that this could impinge on the process too much, and that this impact is not balanced out by the needs of the enquiry? We would suggest that this would mean the use of an observation schedule and a third party observer. In other words, observation completed by someone who is not an actor in the discussion or activity, but that the students are used to having in the classroom and will therefore not overly impact on the actual learning taking place. We would suggest that a possible observation schedule would be one that looks explicitly at cognitive skills, such as the one shown in Table 3.3.

This observation schedule is based upon cognitive skills identified in Moseley et al.'s (2005) model of thinking. The observation schedule allows a record to be made of eight children's participation in learning over time,

Class:

Subject:

Additional Notes

	Cognitive Skills											
	Information Gathering		Basic Understanding					Productive Thinking			
Child ABCDEFGH	Perceptual skills	Accessing stored or recorded knowledge	Adding to and representing meaning	Working with patterns and rules	Concept formation	Organising ideas	Reasoning	Understanding causal relationships	Systematic enquiry	Problem-solving	Creative thinking
	IA / P	IA / P	IA / P	IA / P	IA / P	IA / P	IA / P	IA / P	IA / P	IA / P	IA / P
Apparatus–curriculum based											
Assess peers/self											
Child addressing class											
Collaborating (groups)											
Collaborating (pairs)											
Construction											
Drawing/Painting											
Design											
Drama											
Games–curriculum											
Investigations											
Listening											
Looking											
Movement for task purposes											
Movement PE											
Music or singing											
Problem solving											
Reading aloud											
Reading silently											
Recording work at desk											
Recording work at PC											
Talking to teacher (inc.Q & A)											
Writing at whiteboard											
ADDITIONAL NOTES											

Child A	Child B	Child C	Child D
Child E	Child F	Child G	Child H

Figure 3.3 Observation schedule looking at cognitive skills

looking at the type of activities they are involved in and the type of cognitive skills which they use. It does need a third person to be completed effectively, but as before, pupils could be asked for their reflections on the findings thus increasing the validity.

Pupil's thinking and beliefs

Pupils' thinking behind observed behaviour and behind evidence of learning is the third section which we want to explore in this chapter. In comparison to previously described data, this section could be criticised as being characterised by 'soft' data: data which relies on the pupils' honest appraisal and explanation of 'what is going on in their heads'. That is not to say this data is any less important than other types; indeed, we would argue that it provides an invaluable complementary data source which adds depth to any enquiry. As you will probably have noticed throughout this chapter it has regularly been proposed that pupils should be consulted on quantitative data to find out possible rationales as to why it occurred. For example, on-task/off-task observation data, video footage, self-assessment and national test scores can all stand alone, but if used as a starting point for dialogue with pupils then the reasons behind a particular outcome might start to become clear.

Talk is fundamental to all classrooms and therefore to open up a dialogue about an aspect of teaching and learning as part of an enquiry might appear to be a logical step. There are many different ways in which a pupil can be consulted through the medium of talk, but arising from traditional qualitative research methodology, interviewing tends to be the most commonly thought of and recognised, whether with regard to learning (McCallum et al., 2000), school structures (Thomas et al., 1998) or teachers and teaching (Pollard, 1996; Wragg and Woo, 1984). It is also a method that many teachers feel comfortable with. However, it has to be asked at what point does a discussion about learning, for example, become data collection and at what point is it a pedagogical strategy? Can the purposes of each overlap?

Interviews in their purest form consist of a set of questions to be answered verbally either on a one-to-one basis or as part of a group (focus group interviewing – Puchta and Potter, 2004). An example of an interview schedule used to explore student researchers' experiences can be seen in Box 3.3. At a certain level it does not matter whether you are interviewing children or adults, there are certain things that need to be considered as part of any research. These include the level of structure provided in the interview schedule, the method for recording the communication and the way in which the data is to be analysed. However with children, particularly younger ones, there are a number of additional issues to be considered with regard to this method. For example, it is sometimes perceived that the tighter the structure the better, thus leaving less scope for the topic of conversation to go off at a tangent. However, it does depend on the aim of the research. There might be occasions where an unstructured, immediate response is more useful than something which has been prompted for and thoroughly signposted. For example, we have seen successful enquiries where the teacher–researcher has gone into the playground with one key question and asked a random sample of pupils for their immediate response, whereas we have also seen structured interviews being used consistently across a class.

Box 3.3

Interview Schedule Students as researchers

The aim of this interview is to reflect on and explore what it has been like to be involved as a student researcher at your school. We are interested in what you did over the term and a half you have been involved, what changes you think the process has produced and how it affects your feelings about research and school. We're also interested in how the research has happened: the factors that enabled it and also any barriers which might have acted against it.

1 **Describe the process of your research over the last term and a half.**

   a Why do you think the SMT asked you?
   b Before the project started what were you most excited about?
   c Before the project started what were your main worries about the project?
   d How has the research process developed over the project?
   e What would you do differently if you were to do the research again?
   f What do you think should be the next step for the student as researcher group of Heaton Manor?

2 **What do you feel have been the main outputs of the research?**

   a For you?
   b For group of student researchers?
   c For the school?
   d Do you think you have learnt anything new?
   e What skills have you acquired, if any?
   f Do you think you will use the research skills again? When?

3 **You have given presentations on your findings to the SMT, the staff and parents, what did that feel like?**

   a Did you feel like your findings were taken seriously?
   b Do you think there were any differences between these audiences?
   c What were the main worries about doing something like this?
   d What were you most excited about?

4   **What would you say to a teacher who was thinking about initiating a similar student research group to the ones in Heaton Manor?**

    a   What do you think are the advantages of using student researchers?
    b   What do you think are the disadvantages of using student researchers?
    c   What would you advise other students about doing this type of research?
    d   What would you advise another school that wanted to use student researchers?

As a general rule, we would suggest that some kind of predetermined structure is helpful, although it does not have to be characterised through the traditional semi-structured interview schedule, a task or activity can mediate the interview just as successfully.

When interviewing children, however, as an adult, you need to be aware of the impact you can have on the discourse. Teaching is probably the one profession where we routinely ask questions we know the answer to and therefore children become highly accomplished at guessing what the teacher is thinking. There are also well-established understandings of power that exist in schools, especially as represented by the pupil–teacher relationship. Some of these characteristics are impossible to get away from and therefore within your enquiry you need to recognise their existence and then move on, but there are strategies which you can employ to try and lessen the impact. One such strategy might be allocating other pupils the role of interviewer (many of the strategies talked about in this section can be applied to pupil interviewers) or the use of a mediated interview.

The mediated interview is one which is structured or supported by an object or process. With children, particularly young ones, an interview can be more successful if the talk is additional to another task with which they feel familiar, for example a work sheet, an object used as a discussion point or sorting activity (tasks that keep the child in the *comfort zone* of school, but can also be targeted towards the outcome of the enquiry). Theoretically, through mediating an interview, such potential influences as power relationships between pupil and teacher, and 'guess what the teacher wants to know' scenarios can be somewhat avoided.

With pupil views templates (Wall and Higgins, 2006) the template designed is a 'semiotic tool' (Vygotsky, 1978) and forms the basis of the interview about the teaching activity. By providing an image of the learning situation on which the research is focusing, such as working in a group, or using a computer, the process becomes a three-way interaction between the teacher-researcher, the pupils and the template (see Figure 3.4). The researcher/teacher has an important role within the process of the interview: they initiate the discussion around the chosen learning context and, to a certain extent will steer the dialogue. The template operates as a reminder of the specific learning context under discussion and

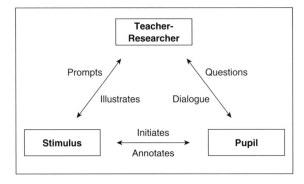

Figure 3.4   Three-way interaction for a mediated interview

thus acts as a stimulus; however, as part of the technique it is annotated by the child and, therefore, becomes a record of the discussion and a stimulus for further talk and elaboration.

The templates have been developed in a cartoon format to help learners to discuss and then record their thinking about learning based on a recent teaching activity. The template design has its inspiration in work completed by the Bubble Dialogue team[1]; for example, McMahon and O'Neill (1992). In this research, speech and thought bubbles were used to support discussion and role play in citizenship and values education. The research of Hanke (2001) was also influential in the design; here thought bubbles were used to gather pupil views of the different sections of the Literacy Hour. The key idea in all these projects is that pupils can be asked, using a cartoon representation, to reflect on their thinking on different aspects of their experience and to undertake a task which is broadly familiar to them in terms of what they usually do in school. This led us to design templates which can help to stimulate reflection on the processes of thinking in different learning contexts.

This method aims to gather information on pupils' attitudes and beliefs about teaching, curriculum content and school/classroom structures (the process of teaching), but also to go further into metacognition and their descriptions of the process of learning. This is done through the common superimposed structure of speech and thought bubbles added to the cartoon representation of the learning context. The thought bubble is intended to look at the 'internal' processes: the learning of the individual – 'what is going on inside their head'. In contrast, the speech bubble looks at factors external to the individual: the learning of other pupils, teachers and parents and practicalities of learning in the specified context. An overlap between the two fields is expected with regard to advantages and disadvantages and subject differences: the impacts on the learning of themselves and others. A diagram of this rationale is shown in Figure 3.5. Therefore, the template appears to have the potential to bridge the world between the concrete descriptions of their learning and the more abstract thinking about what they have learned; in this sense it is a mediating tool.

The templates have usually been used with groups of four to six pupils, much like a focus group interview (Greig and Taylor, 1999). The discussion starts around

paired work

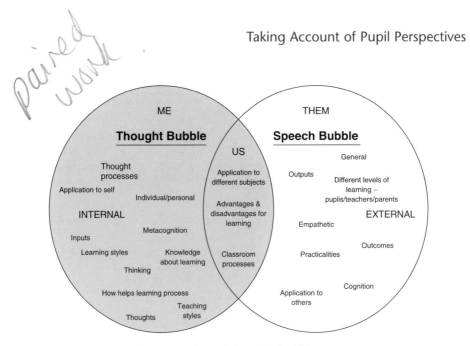

Figure 3.5   Rationale for speech and thought bubble

the template, but the flexibility of the image also means that the learner can add to the picture, for example, by adding in faces and expressions to the teacher and pupils or by drawing representations of their favourite lesson. This approach helps to lessen the tension between interviewer and young person being interviewed by providing them with a familiar task (completing a 'worksheet' see Figure 3.6) that they can get on with as they talk (Greig and Taylor, 1999).

Ideas from the discussion are recorded on the template. Throughout the interview pupils are reminded and encouraged to write down their thoughts and ideas in the appropriate bubble. However, we usually emphasise that they do not need to worry about writing conventions (for example spelling or grammar) but should complete the template in their own way: some pupils have independently used one speech bubble for positive and one for negative impacts on learning; others added their own bubbles for extra space; and a few used drawings to illustrate their meaning. An example of a how a template was used can be seen in the example from Fleecefield Primary School, Enfield.

The Possibilities for Paired Learning in the Primary School

Emma Glasner and Ulfët Mahmout

Fleecefield Primary School, Enfield

Hypothesis

We believe that gender, ability and friendship focused paired work will create a more articulate, emotionally safer environment and improve children's academic performance.

Figure 3.6   Examples of pupil views templates

Research process

To complement the observations we used a 'Pupil Views Template' (see above). We chose one which would enable the children to express the kind of talk they had experienced in the morning's lessons. It was presented to the children in the same way in both classes using the same language, asking the children to reflect on lessons in the morning covering the same content.

Results

In control class none of the children related the children in the picture responses to the lesson on *Goodnight Mr Tom*. In fact, one child imagined it had been a Spanish lesson. For example:

'Hmm, what's that number on Amelia's worksheet? I'll never pass if I do it myself.'

   It appears they were predominately concerned with passing tests and many of the thoughts they ascribed to the template were about rewards or unrelated activities like football and discos. (An example of this association between grades and rewards can be seen in the template completed by a child in the control class included below.)
   Within the control class, there was little or no interaction between the two children shown in the picture and where thoughts were related to the other child, they seemed in competition with each other.
   In the paired learning class all the templates reflected the lesson that they had participated in that morning. The characters in it were always conversing

with each other and working together. They made explicit references to how they were working things out and who was responsible for the various roles within their partnership.

They also ascribed value to their partner in their thoughts and some mentioned how it enabled them to achieve or enjoy the work:

'Do you need help? OK, let's work together.'

What this shows us is not that, if asked specifically, Indigo children, in the control class, could not talk about their learning, and/or, never learn from their peers. But rather that paired learning in the Lilac Class, the experimental group, had created an environment where that kind of talk and knowledge about how you work, your strengths and weaknesses is required. Thus it becomes something you draw upon without being pressed for it.

Developing feedback loops

Researching the pupils' perspective of learning and teaching can be a rewarding and insightful aspect of any enquiry. Since the rise of the pupil voice agenda in schools, teachers are finding that all pupils, regardless of age, can have useful things to say about their experiences of school, teaching and learning. However, we would argue that there is a need to make sure that the process is truly authentic and to do this the process needs to be as transparent as possible.

Throughout this chapter we have emphasised the need to open up the evidence to the pupils, and even where it has been collected without their full participation, there is a rationale for getting their perspective on the outcome. In other words, by asking the pupils about the data which has been collected about them, for example, attendance figures, behaviour observations and work samples, then you add a further dimension to your enquiry and validate the interpretations that you are making. Ultimately, this means opening up the research process to a sustained dialogue about learning and teaching and it is important that this dialogue not only includes other adults, but also pupils. In this way not only will your enquiry be fuelled by different perspectives, but also the evidence can support a

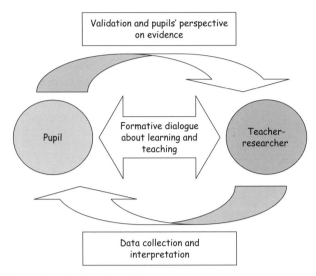

Figure 3.7   Example of a feedback loop

developmental process of thinking and building understanding about learning. This type of feedback loop (see figure 3.7) will then not only benefit your own practice, but also the pupils' thinking about their own learning and development.

Key perspectives on the pupils' point of view

This is a growing area of interest for teachers, policymakers and academics, with some debate about the role of pupils in the process and how far their views inform practice decisions.

Arnot, M., McIntyre, D., Pedder, D. and Reay, D. (2004) *Consultation in the Classroom: Developing Dialogue about Teaching and Learning*. Cambridge: Pearson Publishing.

Clark, J., Dyson, A., Meagher, N., Robson, E. and Wootten, M. (2001) *Involving Young People in Research: The Issues; In Young People As Researchers: Possibilities, Problems, and Politics*. York: Youth Work Press.

Fielding, M. (2001) 'Beyond the rhetoric of student voice: new departures or new constraints in the transformation of 21st century schooling?', *FORUM* 43(2): 100–110.

Flutter, J. and Ruddock, J. (2004) *Consulting Pupils: What's In It For Schools?* London: RoutledgeFalmer.

Wall, K., Higgins, S. and Packard, E. (2007) *Talking about Learning: Using Templates to Find Out about Pupil Views*. Plympton: Southgate Publishers.

References used in this chapter

Alderson, P. (2000) 'School students' views on school councils and daily life at school', *Children and Society*, 14(2): 121.

Arnot, M., McIntyre, D., Pedder, D. and Reay, D. (2004) *Consultation in the Classroom: Developing Dialogue about Teaching and Learning*. Cambridge: Pearson Publishing.

Black, P. and Wiliam, D. (1998) *Inside the Black Box: Raising Standards Through Classroom Assessment*. London: NFER Nelson.

Clark, S. (2001) *Unlocking Formative Assessment: Practical Strategies for Enhancing Pupils' Learning in the Primary Classroom*. London: Hodder & Stoughton.

Clark, C., McQuail, S. and Moss, P. (2003) *Exploring the Field of Listening to and Consulting Young Children*. London: DfES Publications.

Claxton, G. (2004) *Teaching Children to Learn: Beyond Flatpacks and Fine Words (Burning Issues in Education)*. Brimingham: National Primary Trust.

Flutter, J. and Ruddock, J. (2004) *Consulting Pupils: What's In It For Schools?* London: RoutledgeFalmer.

Greig, A. and Taylor, J. (1999) *Doing Research with Children*. London: Sage.

Hanke, V. (2000) 'Learning about literacy: children's versions of the literacy hour, *Journal of Research in Reading*, 23(3): 287–97.

Mcmahon, H. and O'Neill, W. (1992) 'Computer-mediated zones of engagement in learning', in: T. M. Duffy, J. Lowyck and D. H. Jonassen (eds) *Designing Environments for Constuctive Learning*. New York: Springer-Verlag. pp 29–50.

McCallum, B., Hargreaves, E. and Gipps, C. (2000) 'Learning: the pupils' voice', *Cambridge Journal of Education,* 30(2): 275–89.

Moseley, D., Baumfield, V. M., Elliott, J., Higgins, S., Miller, J., Newton, D. and Gregson, M. et al. (2005) *Frameworks for Thinking*. Cambridge: Cambridge University Press.

Ofsted (2003) *The Framework for Inspecting Schools in England from September 2003*. Available at: http://www.ofsted.gov.uk/publications/index.cfm?fuseaction= pubs.displayfile& id =1247&type=pdf (accessed 29 September 2006)

Osler, A. (2000) 'Children's rights, responsibilities and understandings of school discipline', *Research Papers in Education*, 15(1): 49–67.

Pollard, A. (1996) 'Playing the system: pupil perspectives of curriculum, assessment and pedagogy', in, P. Croll (ed.), *Teachers, Pupils and Primary Schooling: Continuity and Change*. London: Cassell.

Puchta, C. and Potter, J. (2004) *Focus Group Practice*. London: Sage.

Raymond, L. (2001) 'Student involvement in school improvement: from data source to significant voice', *FORUM,* 43(2): 58–61

Thomas, S., Smees, R. and Boyd, B. (1998) *Valuing Pupil Views in Scottish Schools,* Policy Paper No. 3, The Improving School Effectiveness Project. London: Institute of Education.

Tunstall, P. and Gipps, C. (1996) 'Teacher feedback to young children in formative assessment: a typology', *British Educational Research Journal,* 22: 389–404.

United Nations Convention on the Rights of the Child (1989) *UN General Assembly Resolution 44/25*. Available online at: www.unhchr.ch/html/menu3/b/k2crc (accessed 12 June 2005).

Vygotsky, L. S. (1978) *Mind in Society: The Development of Higher Psychological Processes*. Cambridge, MA: Harvard University Press.

Wall, K. and Higgins, S. (2006) 'Facilitating and supporting talk with pupils about metacognition: a research and learning tool', *International Journal of Research and Methods in Education*, 29(1): 39–53.

Worrall, S. (2000) *Young People as Researchers: A Learning Resource Pack*. London: Save the Children/Joseph Rowntree Foundation.

Wragg, E. and Woo, E. K. (1984) 'Teachers' first encounters with their classes', in E. Wragg (ed.) *Classroom Teaching Skills*. London: Croom Helm.

Note

1 http://www.dialogbox.org.uk/BubbleDialogue.htm

4

Exploring Your Own and Your Colleagues' Professional Knowledge

CHAPTER CONTENTS

- Importance of the action research cycle for promoting reflection
- Methods and tools for looking at your own practice
- The impact of enquiry on teachers' practice
- Developing collaborative teacher enquiry in schools.

Introduction: What do teachers know? Making 'practical knowledge' explicit

Teachers are experts in a series of inter-related areas of knowledge and practice: they know a great deal about learning, about classroom management, about the curriculum, about ways to communicate their understanding to pupils, about the relationships with learners that promote better motivation and attainment, about the environments they work in within the school and the communities they serve which surround it. Each teacher organises this mass of content and processes knowledge, this collection of experience and theory, in their own unique way. The professional work of teaching does not have a single unifying theory, nor one dominant form of practice (Simon, 1999) rather, it is a patchwork of teachers' experiences, incorporating policy directives and inspection criteria alongside personal beliefs about 'good practice' and the meaning and purpose of teaching as a career (Day et al., 2006). These patchworks are strongly influenced by the school culture in which the teacher works and they may also be embellished by transformative experiences in the teacher's career: a challenging class or individual pupil, an influential mentor or a significant learning experience in continuing professional development (Cordingley et al., 2003; 2005). Each patchwork represents an individual teacher's 'practical knowledge' or 'knowledge in action' (Wien, 1995), some of which is explicitly articulated and some of which is automatic and unexamined.

How do teachers make decisions about what to teach, when and how? How can they create a 'working space' (Clement and Vandenberghe, 2000) to explore what they know, what seems to be successful, what are the areas of doubt and ambiguity? Though there is a great deal in the academic literature about the importance of the 'reflective teacher' (for example, Beijarrd et al., 2004), it is important to examine what it is we mean when we use this term and how reflection is used by teachers to examine their patchwork of ideas, strategies and experience and to select the best tools for each occasion. Teachers are problem-solvers, constantly reacting to the needs of the learners in front of them, assessing the success of lessons or interactions and bombarded by information and competing demands. There is, therefore, a significant risk that reflection may be fragmented: short-term, narrowly focused and driven by outside agendas. Teachers may benefit from a broader perspective on their work, to re-connecting with their core values and purpose; but how likely is it that time will be spent in the staff-room or classroom musing 'Why are we here?', when the immediate and pressing answer is 'To prepare for year 9 after lunch and to mark year 7's homework, to explain to Tony that conflict resolution through escalated violence is not the route advocated by the school and to make sure the bus has been booked for the field trip?'

This chapter suggests that the action research cycle is one, very effective, way in which teachers can achieve reflection that is both sufficiently embedded in the day-to-day needs of practice and sufficiently distanced from the 'taken for granted' to be a lever for change. The structure of the chapter begins with a focus on the teacher-researcher looking at her own practice, followed by a section on eliciting, sharing and interpreting practical knowledge with colleagues and concluding with a discussion of how enquiry in schools can spark changes in practice.

What do you want to know about your own practice?

By undertaking an enquiry in your own classroom, you are inevitably embarking on an examination of some aspects of your own practice. What you are going to do and how you do it are key elements in the research and need to be clearly identified in your research question. (A detailed discussion of the development of your research question can be found in Chapter 2.)

There are two broad types of investigation that you might undertake, depending upon whether your initial approach to action research is focused or exploratory. These can be understood in terms of whether you're asking 'what's happening?', which implies a descriptive exploration of interactions currently going on in your classroom; or whether you're asking 'what happens if?', which indicates that you are planning to make a change or series of changes and to measure their impact. Your action research project may have a 'what's happening?' phase, which generates a 'what happens if?' question, or you may begin with a focused evaluative question, which then reveals the need to look more widely at the variety of factors which influence the area you want to change.

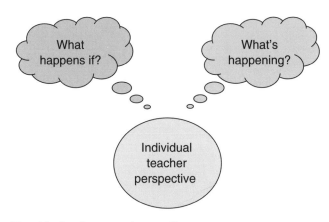

Figure 4.1   Two kinds of research question

Example

A teacher in a small (one form entry) primary school had a very focused project looking at the effect of a change in the way she taught the Victorians, using more source material and drama, on the quality and quantity of writing that her class produced. The motivation for this focus was not simply the desire to improve the writing outputs but also to inject some personal motivation for herself into a topic she had always found rather dull. The findings from the first cycle were rather complex: children from both the higher and the lower ability groups both showed greater enjoyment and motivation and produced longer, more complex and more interesting written work that their previous performance might have predicted. However, a significant group of middle ability children appeared to find the drama work in particular distracting and the quality of their written work did not improve as much as the other groups. In the next phase of the research cycle, the teacher audio-taped sections of her history lessons and compared them with tapes of the literacy hour: what became apparent was that her contributions in the literacy lessons offered more structure and guidelines of the connections between tasks. This led her to wonder if the improvements in history were mainly due to increased motivation and that her middle ability children's performance was more dependent on having the connections between drama and writing made more explicit, thus generating her next research question.

It's perhaps obvious to say that changes in the classroom will be uneven in their effects and that it is very difficult to attribute simple cause and effect. Nevertheless, it is vital to consider this when identifying a question, particularly in relation to the *intent* of the enquiry (see Chapter 1 for a discussion of action research and intent). If you set out to change performance then the markers you look for will be in relation to that performance – be it writing, questioning or scores on a maths test – and you can easily generate an understanding of what change might look like. If you find these changes, having intended to cause them, it is very tempting to assume that you have indeed 'made this happen'. However, classrooms are not sealed containers and even if they were, the contents are so diverse and the interactions between all the elements – the people, the ideas, the emotions, the environment – are so complex that being clear about what might be *the* cause of an observed change is almost impossible. For this reason, it is important to have elements of 'what's happening?' incorporated into the most focused of 'what happens if?' projects in order to show your awareness of this complexity. This is another element in the argument for a mixed methods approach to classroom enquiry which is discussed in depth in Chapter 3.

Tools for exploring 'what's happening?'

These kinds of research tools need to be relatively 'light touch' in terms of the time and effort spent in gathering them, since they need to be repeated over time and they need to be re-visited and reviewed by the researcher. They will still require a regularity of use and a discipline in order to build up a meaningful set of data, but the reward will far outweigh the effort. Having a record of your thoughts, your intentions, your actions and your words to reflect upon releases you from the reliance on your memory, from the distortions of looking back from a position of knowing how it turned out, and allows you to see how your understanding has developed over time.

Diaries and research logs

A research log provides a day-to-day record of what you *do* in a project and is an essential record of why, for example, you only have three observations from the sixth week of the project (Sarah had chicken pox) or why you decided to bring forward the post-test for the year 8s (so as not to include times when some of the classes had student teachers). Keeping an accurate research log is as much a part of good research practice as taking the register and marking work is of good teaching practice.

A research diary is something more. Ideally, it is a supplementary part of the log, so that what you are *thinking* and *feeling* are fully integrated with what you are doing. For this reason, it is important to have a book which you can carry around with you, making notes on the hoof. Better to have lots of phrases and thoughts scribbled in break time regularly than to have one or two full accounts dutifully written at a desk. When we are working with teachers engaged in action research, they sometimes put forward the view that their thoughts and feelings are not 'proper data', in the way that test scores or questionnaires are. We feel very strongly and argue passionately that this is not the case: the intention, motivation and affective states of all the people involved in the project are important aspects which have a role to play in success and failure. Throughout the book we will offer tools which may help you to tap into the thoughts and feelings of students, parents and other professionals. It is, if anything, more important to be aware of your own thoughts and feelings as the research progresses. As the designer and evaluator of the project, there is a natural tendency to see yourself as 'outside the experiment' but clearly if you teach the same lesson to one group feeling fit and energetic and then repeat it with another group with a crushing headache there may well be a different impact. There may well also be patterns in your working week that you are not consciously aware of which the diary will reveal: the Wednesday afternoon slump is well known but there are others, for example, some teachers report that they respond to an energised class coming from a PE lesson.

The research diary can also include longer observations which strike you as important during the research process: notes of group interactions, notes about behaviour, reflections upon conversations with individual students about their learning, reflections on your own role in plenary discussions. You may not have included student interviews in your research design but records of informal conversations are still useful data, giving support or challenge to your other findings. It is important to report this kind of data accurately – as unprompted informal feedback recorded in research notes, rather than as interview data – so that your research audience can make their own judgement about how to weigh it, but is also important to include it as part of the real experience.

Audio and video taping

The research log, supplemented by your lesson plans and assessments, gives a baseline account of what has been done in the enquiry. These are records of your intention and reports of outcomes, supplemented by your memories and, for many projects, they will be sufficient. However, if you are asking a 'what's happening?' question, you may need a broader data collection tool which will scoop up the unexpected as well as the indicators you're looking for. The use of audio and video taping can be very helpful, though there are some important ethical and practical considerations to grapple with.

Video footage is classified as 'personal data' under the Data Protection Act 1998, so it is therefore essential to consider the '3 Ps': Privacy, Permission and Purpose. It is essential to comply with (or negotiate amendments to) your school's policies in relation to the use of video recording during lessons. It may be that the use of video in lessons is covered by a generic letter signed by parents when their children start at the school, if not you will need to get written permission for the specific purpose of gathering video evidence for research. The permission letter should reassure parents that the video is not going to be seen by third parties (in or out of school), and that it will not be used for secondary purposes (for example at a conference, or using stills in a publication) without further permission being sought. There may be some pupils for whom the school does not have permission to make video recordings and in such cases you need to seek advice before proceeding. It is not usually the case that these pupils may not be present during video recording, but you need to consider where they are seated in relation to what the video will capture. Recordings of them speaking as part of the lesson are not restricted in the same way as visual images. Although the use of video is becoming more common in many schools, it can still be a sensitive issue and teachers involved in research may also need reassurance about the privacy attached to the use of video evidence. This can be complicated by the power relations between the teacher being videoed and the teacher collecting the evidence – it is of critical importance to assure teachers that the video is evidence which contributes to answering your research question, not evidence of their performance or in any way an assessment.

In practical terms, you will need to think about the kind of equipment you have access to and how that will affect your research: there are different technical problems in using either digital or analogue-recorded footage (including copying, storing, ease of use when analysing and reflecting). People do get used to being videoed, but you can expect some distraction on the first occasion, so a 'dry run' is a good idea. The less obtrusive the camera is the better – even if that compromises some of the video quality: static cameras on tripods or filing cabinets cause less disturbance than a hand-held one. If you have a general question about interaction or process in the lesson, there is very little reason to move the camera around during the lesson, although there may be occasions when you want to capture more focused information. You need to be realistic about what you will be able to see and hear on the recording – audio quality is rarely very good and if your focus is the detailed content of student responses, you may need to have the 'belt and braces' approach of having audio recorders on the desks as well.

Audio recordings are useful if your focus is on classroom discourse. Tapes can enable you to analyse the detail both of what you said and how you said it, to count the response time you give to students or to assess the contributions and dynamics operating in collaborative groups. In the last example, there is the additional advantage of gathering data at a distance: though the presence of the recorder will have a slightly inhibiting effect on a group, this is nothing to the inhibition caused by an observer with a notebook and an eager expression.

Audio recordings have the advantage of being technically less complex than video to manage and of posing fewer legal and ethical problems. However, it is still important to refer to the '3 Ps'; assure the class and their parents that you will

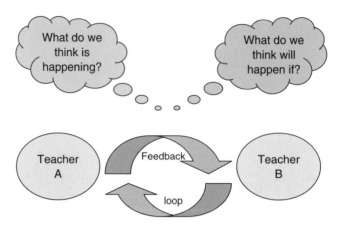

Figure 4.2   Answering research questions with a colleague

store the tapes securely to protect their privacy, that you will not use the recordings or transcripts to identify individuals or groups without their permission and in general, make clear the overall purpose of the data gathering and the research project. On a practical note, check how well your microphone is working (particularly if using a separate desk mike which, as one of the authors found to her cost, needs to be switched on separately) and be aware of other environmental noise – from other groups, from heating, air conditioning and ICT equipment or in the summer from the inevitable lawnmower outside the window.

Observations by a trusted colleague

The previous section focused on methods which are relatively self-contained in that you can manage the data collection without outside assistance. Sometimes, however, it is helpful to have another person's perspective on an interaction or approach. If that other person is a trusted colleague, with their own unique combination of skills, knowledge and experience, this can be a very fruitful source of feedback. It is better to get someone to observe in 'real time', but this is not always possible, so you may ask them to review video or audio recordings.

You need to make a distinction in your own mind and in the mind of your observer between this kind of research observation and the other kinds of peer-to-peer observation which may take place in your school for management, professional development or curriculum development purposes. Therefore, if your question is a 'what will happen if' type, you should have a very specific set of outcomes or changes that you are looking for and your observer will be aware of them. On the other hand, a 'what's happening?' type of question might call for an observation which is very open and which doesn't have many specific parameters. In both cases, your observer's data is meant to be descriptive: what they saw and heard that seems to them to be significant in relation to your research question.

Their data is not meant to be formative: this is not a coaching session intended to directly improve your performance either as a teacher or a researcher. Though there will be things you both pick up on, it is important that the observer does not engage in trying to critique your approach or provide you with moral support – their purpose is to give you another pair of researcher's eyes.

Example

A teacher in a secondary school, engaged on a study of the impact of collaborative group work on students' understanding of scientific concepts, used audio recordings of groups at work on problem-solving and experimental activities. Her own initial analysis focused on the extent to which the groups were actually collaborating and she constructed a series of tables reflecting the amount of each individual's contribution, the length of their utterances and so on (see Table 4.1 below)

Table 4.1   **Data Collected on Group Interaction (11 minute recording)**

Name	Number of utterances	Range of lengths	Mean length	Total length
Ben	14	5–25 secs	6 secs	1 min 30 secs
Shamin	20	5 secs–1min 25 secs	11 secs	3 mins 40 secs
Tara	9	5–30 secs	7 secs	1 min 4 secs
Chris	18	20 secs–1min 5 secs	11 secs	3 mins 10 secs
Hassan	12	5–30 secs	10 secs	2 mins

(Totals do not sum exactly to 11 minutes because participants talk over one another)

Looking at her data the teacher was rather disappointed that the group was dominated by Chris and Shamin, and with the levels of input from the other three, whom she considered had the ability and content knowledge to make more of a contribution. She shared her concern with a colleague who offered to listen to the tape. Her take was quite different: she didn't try to count the number or length of utterances, but was struck by the high quality of the scientific language used and the relative sophistication of the discussions. She pointed out that all participants used the language and that many of the shorter contributions were taking the understanding on or introducing appropriate language (see transcript excerpt below).

(Continued)

> *Chris*: So we've sussed that bit out, OK, now we've got to (uhmmm) look at how the thing changes, how it turns from a solid into a gas when it's heated.
>
> *Tara*: Sublimates.
>
> *Chris*: Yeah, that's right. So, have we got the experiment results on the temperature and what it looked like?
>
> Her colleague's perspective helped the teacher to realise that group work was having an effect but that individual contributions to the process differ. Data collection later in the project revealed that the quality of written work had increased throughout the class. The teacher concluded that there seemed to be beneficial impacts both from listening and of having listeners as a spur to better understanding.

Tools for exploring 'what happens if?'

This kind of enquiry is closest to a classical experimental design since you are introducing a new element into your teaching and learning environment and watching for changes that you can attribute to it. Many teachers involved in action research are concerned that their enquiry is not sufficiently 'scientific' if they do not have control groups or if the comparison classes are not precisely matched to the experimental ones. The issue for us is one of clarity: the rigour and validity of your enquiry rests on how well you report what you have done and how much weight you place on your findings. For example, to report that 'Achievement in maths rose by 20%' needs to be contextualised (see Table 4.2 for a few possible examples) – clearly the kind of measure and comparison is dependent on the focus of your original research question.

Ipsative (self-referenced) comparisons are commonly used in classroom enquiry since the driver for your project is likely to be improving outcomes for your students. It is perfectly valid to report the gains that your students have made and to make reference to how far they have exceeded your predictions (if applicable) provided that you do not, even implicitly, claim that your intervention has definitely been the factor which made this difference. If you are doing a peer comparison, it is important to include as much information as possible about how similar or different the groups are and, for a cohort comparison, whether there were significant factors in the previous year(s), such as building work disruption at the school, staff changes or a greater than normal change in pupil movement which could have had an impact. Peer or cohort comparisons will allow you to make slightly stronger claims about your intervention's role in the observed improvement, though you should be wary of attributing simple cause and effect.

Table 4.2   Ways of Reporting Data

Achievement in maths rose by 20%	Compared to?	Based on?	Over time?
Ipsative (group)	Previous performance of this group	Scores on maths test	One term
Ipsative (individual)	Individual performances	Scores on homework assignments	Two terms
Comparative (cohort)	Last year's Year 6	SATs results	Snapshot
Comparative (peer)	The other Year 6 class who didn't do the intervention	SATs results	One year

The case study from Wilbury Primary school shows how the use of comparison classes can be used to support the project's ipsative findings.

To What Extent is the Development of Speaking and Listening Skills a Prerequisite for Children to become more Efficient Learners?

Ann Mulcahy and Elaine Saini

Wilbury Primary School, Enfield

Hypothesis

This research project aims to explore the hypothesis that the development of speaking and listening skills improves the children's attitudes to learning, behaviour and their capacity to evaluate their learning.

Research process

We realised that a key factor necessary for success was the development of the children's ability to talk about how, as well as what, they were learning. This led to the primary focus being a specific development of speaking and listening. We ensured that observational evidence, including that from the pupils themselves, was collected early on and throughout the year. This was in addition to the continued use of pupil templates and analysis of attainment and behavioural data.

A programme of skills to encourage talk and to improve the quality of paired work and feedback was undertaken with the project class of Year 3 children while the other three Year 3 classes acted as a comparison group.

(For full details of the project please see http://www. campaignforlearning. org.uk/pdf/L2L/Casestudies 2005_ 06/Wilbury.pdf)

Positive, supportive paired relationships had developed over the year, with a reduction in negative comments and a greater understanding of how to work together, evidenced by their own accounts and Pupil Views Templates. Children of all ability levels were found to be using sentences of greater length and of greater complexity by the year's end. The children were also able to complete observations of one another's talk and to identify key features of feedback.

Increase in Average Point Scores between the Comparison Classes and the Project Class

	Project Class [30 children]	Comparison Classes [90 children]
Reading	5.6	2.2
Writing	5.4	3.3
Mathematics	2.5	2.0

At the start of the year the project class was seen as the class with the lowest attainment as adjudged by the SAT results, yet by the end they were the class who had made the most progress.

Results

- The strategies used improved children's speaking and listening skills as well as giving them the language and ability to talk about their own learning.
- There would seem to be a clear link between this development of speaking and listening and the raising of attainment.
- The development of a positive ethos within the class, inherent in the L2L approach, may have supported improvements in the children's behaviours.
- Underlying any of these successful outcomes was the need for the teacher to be knowledgeable, enthusiastic and committed to L2L approaches.

For all of these approaches it is important to take early 'baseline' measures using testing or observations: the earlier, the better. Even if you have not finalised your research question, a general observation or video taken early in the year can be re-analysed to yield specific data about behaviours, questioning or group processes later on. Similarly, broadly focused tests of ability which you would probably do with a new group as part of ongoing planning and assessment can do a double duty as baseline research data. A particular advantage of early baselining is that you have the maximum gap between your pre- and post-tests: since change can take some time to embed and become 'visible' to testing, you are giving yourself a greater chance to measure the effects.

An important consideration is the number of repeat tests or observations you plan to complete and this will, in part, depend on how complex or onerous your research tools are to complete and analyse (see Chapter 3 for an extended discussion of pupil observation tools). However, the rate of change and the kinds of change that happen will differ according to your focus: it is likely that for an enquiry with a strong attainment or outcome focus you will need fewer repeat measures than for an enquiry which is exploring process, motivation or behaviour. If you do undertake a series of observations, it is vital that you include an element of personal reflection: are you absolutely clear about what you are observing and the characteristics you are using to define it and are you aware of how much you are impacting on the observation?

Example

Two relatively inexperienced researchers were working in a school as part of a project looking at classroom discourse and spent a morning in Year 5 classes, observing plenaries in the Literacy Hour and coding the teacher's questions. Henry enthused that his session included lots of open questions, while Joe bemoaned the fact that there were hardly any in his. Later the project team conducted an exercise in inter-rater reliability, where everyone watched the videos of the plenaries and codes the questions. The more experienced team members coding differed, but not very widely, and tended to rate both classes as having similar levels of open questions. As the discussion developed, it became clear that Henry had been basing his coding on his interpretation of the teacher's *intent* when asking the question and Joe was using his assessment of the pupils' *response.* The vexed question of what an open question actually might be is still being addressed elsewhere (Smith and Higgins, 2006), though in the meantime, the team developed a tighter working definition.

What do you want to find out about other teachers?

You may have a research question which goes beyond your own practice or your own classroom: you may be engaged on a collaborative enquiry across a curriculum team or within a year group or key stage or your question might be focused more upon variations in professional practice. These questions draw upon our understanding of shared expertise and can help us to make more explicit the context of our individual schools and the communities of practice (Lave and Wenger, 1991) which operate there.

If your research question is focused on the way other teachers approach a particular area of practice – a 'what's happening elsewhere?' question – then one of your key research tools will be observation. All of the considerations discussed earlier apply, with the additional factor of your role as observer and the power relations between you and the teachers that you are observing. It is self-evident that a teacher will have a different view of you coming in to her classroom to observe (or watching a video of her practice) depending on whether you are relatively junior to her and apparently 'watching to learn' or relatively senior to her and 'watching to critique'. The key to overcoming these natural fears is absolute clarity about the intent of your project, the focus of the research and the role that the observation will play. Only then can the teacher give informed consent to being involved and ethical principles demand that this is the only form of consent that is good enough.

More approaches to finding out what other teachers know

Ideally, observations and other data from your colleagues will be explored and enriched through the use of other qualitative methods such as questionnaires, focus groups and individual interviews. A detailed discussion of questionnaire design can be found in Chapter 5 but some special consideration to giving questionnaires to colleagues needs to be addressed here. It is tempting to assume that the purpose of your enquiry is self-evident, and to ask very open-ended questions which require a great deal of writing. This can often backfire in two ways: busy teachers will be reluctant to compose essays about their teaching and the data you do get back will be individual, idiosyncratic and difficult to analyse. Questionnaire design should be extremely focused and aim to elicit mainly factual (How much, how often, when in the term/year?) information. This can then serve as a foundation to explore the more complex questions which relate to motivation (Why this and not another, why at all?) and affect (How does this feel, how do they react?) which are more easily tackled through interviews and focus groups. Questions of time and focus are equally important here: an interview or focus group schedule should have no more than five focused questions or one open question and should not be scheduled to last more than an hour. Audio recording is extremely helpful for both interviews and focus groups, as it allows you to be fully engaged in the conversation and to support and extend the discussion without being distracted by note-taking. Video of focus groups can be useful in identifying individual speakers but if your focus is on exploring a range of views, rather than attributing those views to individuals, it is probably not worth the bother.

Individual interviews enable you to explore issues in depth and afford your interviewee a confidential, safe space to talk about his practice; focus groups will

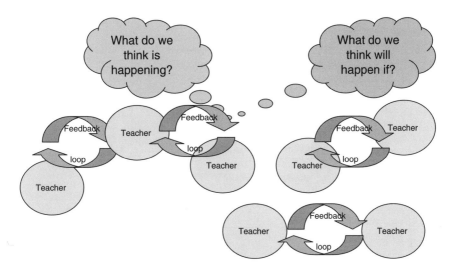

Figure 4.3   The development of a distributed network of enquirers

give you a range of views, enable you to map complementary and opposing views together and have the advantage of many brains attacking the same problem. Individual interviews are time-consuming to conduct and to analyse; focus groups are vulnerable to being hijacked by the most articulate or opinionated participants. Whichever approach you choose, it is good practice to engage your colleagues as co-enquirers rather than research subjects. Always share your interview or group questions beforehand so that people come prepared and engaged and give a reasonable proportion of the time to them to suggest other questions or means of approaching the problem. The quality of your data will be immeasurably improved by your recognition of their expert status and you will be contributing to a culture of mutual support and collaborative working within your school.

In a collaborative enquiry, it is vital to have regular, protected time in which to meet and discuss the progress of the research, the particular problems and techniques associated with different tools and the emerging understanding of the problem. The support of the management team in your school will be needed to give your work the necessary status to 'carve out' this protected time. One of the most common reasons for collaborative enquiries to be less successful is a lack of institutional support.

In our experience of working with teachers engaged in action research we have become aware of a variety of processes which seem to support the development of a community of enquirers. In the initial phases, individual teachers, or small groups begin to work on classroom based projects. They have limited contact with one another about this, often only at the end of a cycle, when findings are shared across the school. This distributed network can offer a level of support and encouragement, but it lacks formal recognition from senior management and the onus is on the

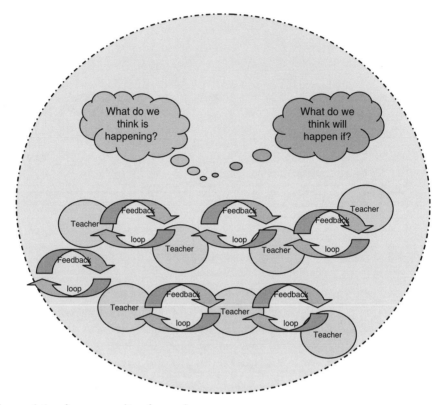

Figure 4.4   A community of enquirers

teachers themselves to share their learning about the process of research, good and bad research tools and the difficulties and triumphs of analysis.

Over time, however, the individuals and groups begin to form a more coherent identity within the school, often with the support of an advocate of enquiry from the management team. Their work becomes less of a fringe activity: they may have more resources and support in terms of time or cover to conduct their research; indeed some schools give bursaries to individuals or groups to support teacher research. This, of course, makes research a more attractive prospect for other teachers in the school and they join in until the school finds itself at a 'tipping point' where sufficient numbers of staff are involved that research is a mainstream activity, which permeates CPD, staff meetings, curriculum and key stage planning. The feedback loops from individual enquiries begin to join up, creating a community of enquirers who can learn from and support one another. Sometimes bigger research projects emerge, though this does not mean that larger enquiries drive out the smaller ones: the individual teacher's autonomy in choosing her focus is the engine which keeps the community ticking over.

Key perspectives on exploring professional knowledge

The context of your own and your colleagues' professional knowledge is an important factor, since the life history of teachers and the circumstances in which they work shape the ways in which they take in, process and adapt new learning.

Cochran-Smith, M. and Lytle, S. L. (2004) 'Practitioner inquiry, knowledge and university culture', in J. J. Loughran, M. L. Hamilton, V. K. LaBoskey and T. L. Russell (eds), *International Handbook of Self-Study of Teaching and Teacher Education Practices*. Dordrecht: Kluwer Academic Publishers.

Frost, D. and Durrant, J. (2003) *Teacher-Led Development Work*. London: David Fulton.

Nias, J. (1989) *Primary Teachers Talking: A Study of Teaching as Work*. London: Routledge.

References used in this chapter

Beijaard, D., Meijer, P. C. and Verloop, N. (2004) 'Reconsidering research on teachers' professional identity', *Teaching and Teacher Education*, 20(2): 107–28.

Clement, M. and Vandenberghe, R. (2000) 'Teachers' professional development: a solitary or collegial (ad)venture?', *Teaching and Teacher Education*, 16: 81–101.

Cordingley, P., Bell, M., Rundell, B., Evans, D. and Curtis, A. (2003) *The Impact of Collaborative CPD on Classroom Teaching and Learning: How Does Collaborative Continuing Professional Development (CPD) for Teachers of the 5–16 Age Range Affect Teaching and Learning?* London: EPPI-Centre.

Cordingley, P., Bell, M., Evans, D. and Firth, A. (2005) *The Impact of Collaborative CPD on Classroom Teaching and Learning: What Do Teacher Impact Data Tell us about Collaborative CPD?* London: EPPI-Centre.

Day, C., Stobart, G., Sammons, P. and Kington, A. (2006) 'Variations in the work and lives of teachers: relative and relational effectiveness', *Teachers and Teaching: Theory and Practice*, 12: 169–92.

Simon, B. (1999) 'Why no pedagogy in England?', in J. Leach and B. Moon (eds), *Learners and Pedagogy*. London: Paul Chapman/Open University. pp. 34–45.

Smith, H. and Higgins, S. E. (2006) 'Opening classroom interaction: the importance of feedback', *Cambridge Journal of Education*, 36(4): 485–502.

Wien, C. A. (1995) *Developmentally Appropriate Practice in 'Real Life': Stories of Teacher Practical Knowledge*. New York: Teachers College Press.

5

Engaging with the Views of Parents and Other Adults

CHAPTER CONTENTS

- Making good use of what you already know about parents and the community
- Methods for learning more about the impact of parents and the wider community on children's learning in your school
- Parents as sources of validation for the outcomes of a cycle of enquiry
- Recruitment of parents as research partners.

Introduction: accessing data beyond the school gates

It will hardly be news to any teacher that the impact of individual schools on children's outcomes is by far outweighed by factors relating to the area they live in (HEFCE, 2005), the ethnicity (Mirza, 2006; Harding, 2006) and socio-economic status of the family, the educational background of the parents and other children in the family (Sacker et al., 2002) and the attitude of the family towards education and the child's achievement (Desforges and Abouchaar, 2003). The last of these factors – family attitudes and support for learning – is at the same time one of the most powerful *and* the only one that schools can realistically engage with. Philosophers and politicians argue that education is an agent for economic and social change but what teachers and schools can achieve does not include the economic regeneration of areas, rather we have to work with communities and families *as they are* and develop ways of communicating so that the goals and aspirations of home and school come closer together and develop dynamically over time.

Many teachers engaged in enquiry have designed questions which are tightly focused on curriculum, classroom interaction and assessing the quality and extent of students' understanding and, for this reason, they do not tend to include collecting data from parents or including parents in the reflection process. When the research cycle is repeated, however, many teachers find that they need this perspective to make sense of their data. To put it in experimental terms, the classroom is not a closed system and any change that is made and evaluated in the classroom needs to take some account of the factors which, while not physically present, have a considerable effect on interactions and outcomes.

> When we looked at our first year results, there seemed to be differences between the children [in performance] that we couldn't explain by looking at their old test scores or their general behaviour and attitude in class. We had sent support materials home and we wondered if that had made the difference – some parents using them, some not. When we asked some of the parents we found that they had mostly been using the games but had really different ideas about what they were for – some of them really good ideas, just different from ours! This year, we're trying to get the parents involved at the beginning, so we're all singing from the same sheet. (KS2 Maths project)

Including parents in your thinking about the action research cycle means taking some time at the outset to explore what you know about parents, what constitutes a reasonable and achievable question or set of questions and how you are going to evaluate the responses that you get, in the same way as you have done before. However, there is a further layer when dealing with parents or the wider community: you have to make a distinction between research purposes. These commonly divide between *validating* the work you have already done with children, *recruiting* parents to the teaching and learning team and *exploring* parents' perspectives (see Figure 5.1).

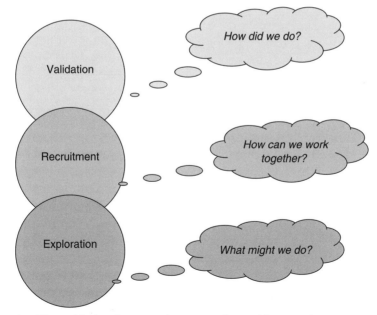

Figure 5.1   Three kinds of research approaches with parents

In validation research, you are essentially asking '*How did we do?*' You need to present your target group of parents with plenty of information about your work in the classroom – not just what you have done but what your underlying intentions were – and provide them with a range of ways to respond to it. You can often do validation after the event, though the data you get will be richer if you start sharing information at the beginning and you will have the opportunity to sample parents' opinions at different points in the process. The tools you'll use will probably be quite focused and may include structured questionnaires or surveys.

In recruiting projects, you are asking parents to become active partners in the business of teaching and learning, asking '*What can we do together?*' The intervention itself involves parents supporting their child's learning through participation at home or at school and will be evaluated through a mixture of methods: the impact on learning or behaviour in school, the reported feelings of students and parents and the quality of communication between parents and teachers. Attainment data, behaviour or attendance records and questionnaire or interview data will be complementary tools in this sort of project.

In exploratory research, you are fundamentally asking '*What might we do?*' Often this represents the next stage in teacher's thinking about working with parents. An initiative may have been validated and had an observable impact on most parents in one year but then have been less successful the next. Alternatively, some parents loved it but others disliked or ignored it – it boils down to the fact that the answers you got from asking '*How did we do?*' weren't simple or satisfactory, instead you may need to find out about the underlying expectations that you and the parents have, to work out how you can get together to achieve the goals of the research. You'll need more open-ended research tools like focus groups and interviews and the role of parents in the process tends to be more active: some of them may come to be 'research partners'.

What do you already know about parents?

Schools collect a lot of information and ask for a lot of feedback, directly and indirectly. Every report that goes home, every letter asking for comments and responses, every open meeting is an opportunity for the school to gather information about parents – their situations, their views, their priorities for their children.

You already know a lot about parents' ideas about the school, though it may not be explicit knowledge. For example, you know whether parents come in to talk to you informally or whether they come in only at your request or theirs to deal with specific issues. This will, in part, be shaped by the policies in your school and the age of children you teach but it is also a piece of information about what your parents think is appropriate in terms of communication. You will also be able to compare your experiences with those of your colleagues – do certain age groups, subject areas or roles within the school attract more contact between home and school? This is particularly important information if you want to increase the levels of communication, since you can be strategic, building on from where relationships are already strong. It is also interesting to canvass your colleagues' opinions about parents: are home–school relationships generally good?; are there specific groups of parents who are more or less 'on-side' than others?; do some kinds of events attract more parents than others? You may be surprised about the diversity of answers you get, even in a small school, but it is important to explore what the school's assumptions about parents are. It may be useful to check up on how the school communicates with parents – do some letters look more 'official' than others?; how many times a year are parents asked for information or opinions already and what are the response rates like? – this will both save you time asking for repeated information and enable you to think critically about how to approach your research question.

You will know, or be able to find out, how many hits your school website gets, how quickly parents sign up for parents' evening meetings and how often these meetings over-run, or how many people are actively involved in volunteering in the school, or – by going through the contact information for your students – you may be able to estimate how many parents are working, or how many students are cared for by the extended family: this could be vital information if you are wanting to have conversations in your project about homework support, for example.

Ways of organising and adding to this data

As far as possible, you need to work with the existing systems used in your school, though some of these will probably be held as electronic files which will make life easier. Setting up monitoring systems *in advance* for homework completion, library books, story sack borrowing or other activities will enable you and other colleagues to gather ongoing data easily. Make good use of the school calendar, so that you have plenty of notice of events where parents will be accessible to you, such as assemblies, open evenings and school fairs, and can plan surveys, questionnaires or focus groups to coincide with them. It is important to spend some time making sure that your data about parents is of reasonable quality: for example, working from an old address list will significantly impact on the number of questionnaire responses you get. When talking to your colleagues, keep an informal note of parents they mention as supportive – these people can be key partners in designing your questions or recruiting other parents.

Feedback loops

As we discuss throughout this book (and particularly in Chapters 1 and 2), one of the principal benefits of action research is the creation of feedback loops for the teacher about teaching and learning as it happens. The feedback loops between home and school vary in size and efficacy because of a range of factors relating to the age of the students, the culture of the school and the relationships between teachers and parents. However, even the twice-daily feedback between parent and teacher in a nursery setting, for example, could be *focused* and *enhanced* by the structure of a research project. Sharing information with parents about an enquiry and seeking regular feedback throughout the project can improve the research questions, re-focus the data collection and inform the analysis.

Doing validation research with parents

This takes your classroom-based action research to a more sophisticated level, recognising the importance of the learning and experience that children have outside school and exploring the extent to which parents can track changes in children's learning or behaviour and triangulate your own findings.

Example

A year one class has been using Community of Enquiry techniques throughout the Spring term to encourage higher order thinking in science and to encourage children to make and support hypotheses about growing plants. The teacher has research data which shows that more than half of the children are talking about plant growth in a more logical and systematic way, that they are able to debate possibilities with one another and that the format of Community of Enquiry appears to be encouraging a small group of children, previously reluctant to speak in large group situations, to make a significantly larger number of contributions. The teacher had sent topic information to parents in September but had not given specific information about the research project or about Community of Enquiry. She conducted a number of informal interviews with parents during the tea and coffee session after the class assembly (on *The Enormous Sunflower*), where she asked them if the children had talked about the science topic at home. She received a certain amount of validation from some of these conversations, but was surprised to learn that several parents mentioned that they felt their children were exhibiting some challenging behaviours at home, particularly using the formula *'I disagree with that because ... '*. An animated discussion sprang up between a group of parents about this, with some expressing concern about 'cheeky' behaviour and others showing pride in the child's 'feisty' stance.

As this example demonstrates, it is important to keep an open mind about the potential impact of an intervention which has specific aims within the classroom but which may produce other results in different contexts. The teacher in this case realised that because she had not made either the purpose or the processes of Community of Enquiry explicit to the parents, children were getting quite variable feedback from home. Moreover, the feedback she was asking for from parents was not based on a shared understanding of what was being evaluated – what change was intended and how it might look or sound.

Useful tools for validation

Short questionnaires

Short questionnaires are a good research tool for repeated use: if your enquiry is tracking changes in behaviour which might be observed at home as well as at school, a short questionnaire can be used to create a baseline and repeated at the end of the project, or at intervals, to track gradual change. When you are asking parents about behaviours, it is a good idea to avoid *'always, frequently, sometimes, rarely, never'* headings for responses, since these are ambiguous: my 'sometimes' could be a lot less than yours. Specific measures, *'more than twice a day, every day, two or three times a week, once a week, less than once a week'*, are easier to understand and also give you a better basis for comparison. A project which reports that before the intervention *'most parents "sometimes" talked about maths at home with their children but afterwards the proportion of those who "frequently" did so rose by a third'* sounds OK but being able to say *'Before the project only 25% of parents said they talked about maths every day and 15% said they talked about it less than once a week. After the "Maths is Everywhere" project, 48% said they talked about maths every day and all parents talked about maths at least once a week'* is both a lot clearer and more impressive.

Short questionnaires are also useful for gathering descriptive data about parents' current ideas or practice. In general, the questions should be clear, short and where possible, allow the respondent to tick a box rather than write a long answer. It is important that the questionnaire does not ask for information you already have or that does not seem relevant to the research question. For example, a project focusing on reading and looking into reading homework might justifiably ask about the range of adults who spend time caring for the child after school, though it would be important to look carefully at the phrasing of the question. Comparing the two examples in Boxes 5.1 and 5.2., which would you react best to?

Box 5.1

Do you help your child with their reading homework?

| Every night | Most nights | Some nights | Never |

If you don't read every night, does someone else do it?
(please specify) _____

Box 5.2

We are looking at how best to organise the reading homework for Class 5. Please fill in the table below so we know what you and your child are doing after school

	Monday	Tuesday	Wednesday	Thursday	Friday
Child looked after by e.g. Mum, Dad, Grandparent, Childminder, After school club					
Other after school activities e.g. Cubs, Brownies, music, sport, other clubs, helping at home					
Good days for reading homework are					

If you are looking for parents' views, you can give them a series of positive and negative statements, to which they can either agree/disagree or give a range of responses on a Lickert scale (*Strongly Agree, Agree, Neither Agree or Disagree, Disagree, Strongly Disagree*). However, we would recommend that you draw these statements from interviews or focus groups (see below) that you have carried out with a smaller group of parents in the school, since it may be a mistake to assume that you can guess what the range of views might be.

A good rule of thumb for a short questionnaire is that it should fit on one side of A4 and be quick to fill in. Bear in mind that if you want to repeat the questionnaire and want to track changes in individuals you will not be able to make them anonymous, though you can give each family a number so that you are not focusing on what you *think* you know about them when you are looking at responses. If you use anonymous questionnaires you will only be able to track changes in the cohort as a whole and if you don't get all of them back, you won't necessarily know if you're comparing the same twenty responses from before and after. However, if you're looking at opinions and not planning to repeat, you may find that you get more responses if parents know they are responding anonymously.

Home–school learner logs

These are a particularly good research tool if you want to set up regular feedback and to develop conversations with parents about learning.

As the examples in Figure 5.2 show, they can be used with very young learners as a way of sharing experiences, using drawings, collage or photographs.

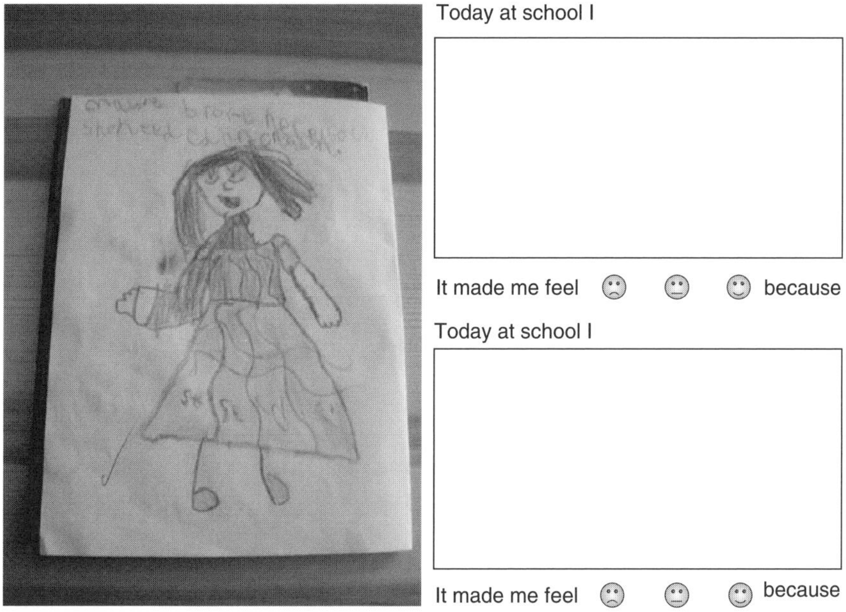

Figure 5.2   Two examples of Home Learning Logs: one completely unstructured, one with a basic drawing structure and a focus on affective and motivational data collection

As learners get older, the focus of feedback can be more specific and can be used to make parents aware of the demands or the language being used in the classroom (see Figure 5.3).

Informal interviews and focus groups

This is probably the most efficient method of gauging parents' opinions, since the organisation of the interviews or focus group is ideally 'piggy-backed' onto a pre-existing event when parents are available, such as an assembly, open evening or sports event. Teachers in primary settings can also experiment with having

UNIVERSITY OF
NEWCASTLE

LEARNER LOG

School: Name:

Date: Lesson:

Outline of lesson

How well do you think you achieved the objectives for the lesson?
(put an X on the line to indicate how you feel)

☺   ☺   ☹

Completely---------------------------- Mostly ------------------------- Not at all

How did you do? (please circle how you feel about how you worked in
each part of the lesson with 1 = extremely well … 5 = not very well
at all or use n/a if it does not apply).

	☺				☹	
Beginning of the lesson	1	2	3	4	5	n/a
Working in a group	1	2	3	4	5	n/a
Working on your own	1	2	3	4	5	n/a
Thinking of ideas	1	2	3	4	5	n/a
Talking about ideas	1	2	3	4	5	n/a
Writing down ideas	1	2	3	4	5	n/a
End of the lesson	1	2	3	4	5	n/a

Any other thoughts?

LEARNING AND ENJOYMENT AUDIT

I don't enjoy this subject	1 2 3 4 5	I really enjoy this subject
I don't find it interesting	1 2 3 4 5	I find it really interesting
I don't see the point/purpose	1 2 3 4 5	I do see the point/purpose
I find it challenging	1 2 3 4 5	It's never a challenge
I have to really think about it	1 2 3 4 5	I don't have to think
I don't have to explain my reasons/answers	1 2 3 4 5	I have to explain my reasons /answers
I/we don't make many connections to other things	1 2 3 4 5	I/we make a lot of connections to other things
I don't talk a lot about the work during lessons	1 2 3 4 5	I talk a lot about the work during lessons

Other comments

Figure 5.3 Two examples of learner logs designed for older students, emphasising process and intention within lessons and making explicit links to metacognition

more flexible time boundaries for parents at the beginning and end of the day, for example having an 'open' story-time to which parents are welcomed, or a collaborative first activity of the day at which parents can stay and participate. Be aware, however, that you are only accessing a limited sample of parents and carers at these events: you will be much less likely to encounter those working full time, for example. You will find it a great advantage if you can offer tea or coffee and biscuits to encourage parents to come and linger and to have a 'briefing sheet' about your enquiry project that parents can look at. Limit yourself to one area of data collection and, if possible, to one key and focused question that parents can reasonably be expected to respond to without preparation. It is far more comfortable for parents to be asked '*Does Tom like the new reading scheme better than the old one?*' – a question that they can easily answer and which may then lead on to them discussing related topics about books, reading and their child than to be asked '*We're putting more emphasis on phonics in our teaching this term – have you noticed a difference in the way Tom spells out words?*' – a question which parents might want to know about in advance, so that they could watch for the change.

Longer questionnaires

Sometimes it is necessary to ask quite a lot of questions of parents. In that case a longer questionnaire, with a mixture of open and closed questions is advisable. Even with a longer format, it is important to make sure that the layout is clear and the categories are relatively unambiguous. If possible, keep the questionnaire to less than four sides and print on both sides of the paper so that parents don't feel they have a huge sheaf of paper to deal with. The example below was created with the teachers at Lanner school in Cornwall as part of the *Learning to Learn* project.

Lanner Parent Questionnaire

About your child's learning at school

1 How confident are you that you know *what* your child is learning at school? *Please tick one box*

Not at all confident	I know some of what is going on	I know most of what is going on	Very confident

2 How do you find out **what** your child is learning at school? *Please tick all that apply*

The school send me letters and leaflets	My child tells me	My child's teacher tells me	I hear about things from other parents	Other (*please state below*)

Other ways of finding out _____

3 How confident are you that you understand **how** your child is learning at school? *Please tick one box*

Not at all confident	I know some of what is going on	I know most of what is going on	Very confident

4 How do you find out **how** your child is learning at school? *Please tick all that apply*

The school send me letters and leaflets	My child tells me	My child's teacher tells me	I hear about things from other parents	Other (*please state below*)

Other ways of finding out _____

5 Would you be interested in finding out more about what and how your child is learning at school? Please tick one box

Yes	No

6 What sort of information or event would you find useful? *Please tick all that apply*

Visiting the school/ watching lessons	Meetings with teachers	After-school events on subjects and learning approaches	More information to read at home	Other (*please state below*)

Other information/event ─────────────────────────

About your child's learning at home

7 Do you agree with the statement 'Learning only takes place at school'? *Please tick one box*

Yes	No

8 Does homework help your child to reinforce his/her learning? *Please tick one box*

A lot	Quite a lot	It depends on the subject (please go to Q.9)	Not very much	Not at all

9 How much does homework help your child to reinforce their learning? *Please tick one box*

	A lot	Quite a lot	Not very much	Not at all
Reading				
Writing				
Maths				
Topic work				

10 Do you help your child with homework? *Please tick one box*

Always	Quite a lot	Not very much	Not at all

11 Do you agree with the statement 'Children should do their homework independently'? *Please tick one box*

Yes	No

12 Do you agree with the statement 'Parents can help their children's learning in a different way from teachers' *Please tick one box*

Yes	No

13 Is your child motivated to complete their homework? *Please tick one box*

Always	Most of the time	Sometimes	Rarely

14 If your child is less motivated sometimes, why do you think this is?
Please tick all that apply

Bored with work	Too busy with other activities	Too tired after school	Homework too hard	Homework too easy	Other school (*please state below*)

Other _____

15 Do you have any other concerns or ideas about learning in our school that you would like to raise? *Please use this space to let us know.*

Recruiting parents to collaborative projects

Teachers have long recognised the benefits of engaging parental support for learning, either through homework support, positive encouragement or active modelling in schools through volunteering. In collaborative projects, the aim is for parents and schools to work together towards a common goal. It is very important to make sure that the project is set up in such a way as to enable parents to have some input into the 'goal setting'. While teachers may identify an area in which they want to target children's motivation and learning, it is an advantage to involve parents early on in the planning stages, rather than presenting them with activities and ideas in a way which could be perceived as patronising. Even if this is not practically possible, the ways in which parents are invited to take part are crucial – avoiding the impression of singling out families of children who are 'struggling', not portraying the parents' role as 'teacher's helper' and more positively, valuing the perspectives of parents. These points are illustrated by two case study examples, one from a primary and one from a secondary school (see pages 92–94). Both of these are good examples of the way in which working together with parents enables a common language about learning and assessment to build up, which then provides better support for students and shows itself in higher levels of motivation, engagement and attainment.

Does Introducing Parents to Learning to Learn Techniques Have a Positive effect on pupils' Achievement?

Linda Stephens, Irene Pooley

St Meriadoc C of E Nursery and Infant School, Cornwall

Hypothesis

We are looking at the role of family learning in supporting Learning to Learn by arranging a series of evenings to introduce parents to the major L2L approaches. We will monitor the impact that the parent's involvement has on the confidence and capability of their children.

Research process

We decided to hold a series of nine sessions for parents. These were held in the school hall every fortnight starting in October and continuing into the Spring Term. We agreed that the best time to hold the meetings was in the evenings so that more people would have a chance of attending.

An initial invitation was sent out which included a paragraph about our involvement in the Campaign for Learning Research Project. We made it clear that although it was not necessary to attend all sessions we would be keeping a register of parents so that we could see whether regular attendance had more effect than just coming to one or two talks.

The topics covered were:

1 Seeing yourself as a learner, which included self talk and neuro-linguistic programming (NLP)
2 Three main ways to learn, VAK and brain gym
3 Overcoming barriers to learning by raising self-esteem
4 Memory skills and techniques to aid memory
5 Visual learning including mind maps
6 The different ways of being intelligent, a brief overview of all of the intelligences
7 Thinking skills, various ways of promoting thinking e.g. by odd one out puzzles, mysteries, fortune lines,
8 The importance of talk in particular using a philosophy with children approach
9 Formative Assessment and reflecting on your own learning.

At the end of each session parents were encouraged to note down anything that they felt they had learnt from that particular session or general comments about how they thought it had gone. At the end of the series of talks parents were issued with a questionnaire to determine how they felt their attendance would benefit their children's learning.

Results

- Sharing Learning to Learn approaches with parents raises their own self-esteem and confidence as learners
- Involving parents in Learning to Learn enables them to feel more able to teach and help their own children at home
- The confidence of the parents communicates itself to the children
- Even after only a few months improvements have been noticed in some of the children's performance.

Assessing the Impact of Getting Parents More Involved in School Programme on Student Motivation and Attainment

John Welham

Camborne Science and Community College, Cornwall

Hypothesis

The project aims to evaluate the impact of a programme in which parents of Year 11 GCSE students were invited to school sessions in and out of school time. The project seeks to involve parents more directly in the work of their children at school in order to sustain and develop student motivation and thus improve attainment.

Research process

Parents were invited to join their children and the Design Technology teachers for two introductory sessions, where they were given the outline of the course and a breakdown of the coursework assignments. They were then introduced to five things that the staff promised to do and five things that students would need to do, before being given a list of five things they could do that would help their children to complete the coursework successfully. This included simple suggestions such as talking to their child about the coursework assignment; making time each week to review their progress; contacting school if they had any concerns; agreeing to support their children's attendance at out of hours sessions.

Parents were then shown an exhibition of selected (successful) samples of the previous year's coursework and the breakdown of the grades for those pieces of coursework.

The parents of just over 80% of the students involved in the project attended this first session.

The next stage was to invite these parents to a DT lesson during school time. They attended a special session, with their children, which modelled the coursework process and helped them to understand how their children were expected to work.

Finally, there was a celebration of coursework evening, open to the whole school community, to which the parents and students were invited.

GCSE coursework scores in Design and Technology and Geography from previous years and GCSE coursework scores, hand-in and completion rates from Design and Technology groups not involved in the project – for comparison data were collected.

Before and after the intervention, data about student performance was collected, including GCSE coursework scores in DT from previous years, GCSE coursework scores and completion rates. Colleagues were interviewed as a follow up measure, while parents and students were interviewed throughout the life of the project and when the coursework was completed.

Results

- The intervention seems to have had a distinct impact on coursework marks, which in turn has impacted on GCSE grades attained.
- Feedback from teachers, students and teachers has been very positive.

Advocacy

Often another goal of projects like these is that groups of parents will act as advocates, drawing in less engaged groups of parents into school activities and creating a wider learning network around the school. This is a process that takes a significant amount of time and relies heavily on the personal qualities of teachers and parents involved, so it is vital not to have too high an expectation of this kind of effect in the early years of a project. Research suggests that the more similar the home and school cultures are, the easier it is to get widespread engagement in a relatively short time (for example, Hall and Santer, 2001). However, in all schools, the population of families constantly changes and it is important to consider outreach and advocacy elements of parental involvement as continually evolving.

Useful tools for collaborative projects

The tools for validation research are equally valid in collaborative projects, in particular the use of learning logs to keep dialogue between home and school ticking over throughout the project. In reflecting on the experience of working together, the use of reasonably short and structured *interviews* is a particularly useful strategy. It may well not be practical to interview all the parents in the project and you will have to decide what criteria you will use to construct a sub-sample. You may have been collecting other data – for example on pupil attainment or confidence – which will provide you with a sampling frame (see example in Table 5.1). This will enable you to talk to a representative group of parents.

Table 5.1   Sampling Frame

Example sampling frame	Children with higher confidence scores	Children with medium confidence scores	Children with lower confidence scores
Parents involved	(Total = 5) 2	(Total = 6) 2	(Total = 2) 1
Parents not involved	(Total = 4) 2	(Total = 7) 2	(Total = 3) 1

You may not have data which is suitable for creating a sampling frame, but you may have conducted a questionnaire, which will allow you to pick out parents with a range of perspectives to explore in more detail in the interviews. Or you may not really know what the issues are for parents and will have to conduct an opportunity sample, where you ask parents to volunteer to discuss the project with you and you work with perhaps a single open question asking them to reflect on their experiences. This is a harder approach to manage because you can only judge when to stop doing interviews when you feel that your research categories from the interviews are 'saturated': that you are not getting any new data from parents.

Interviews need to take place in a quiet place, away from distractions and inter-ruptions, at a time when neither you nor your interviewee has to be somewhere else urgently and can relax and give full attention to the interaction. Again, tea and biscuits are helpful. The interview questions should be shared in advance of the interview, so that there is no feeling of surprise or discomfort. The design of a short interview schedule needs to have no more than five focused questions for a half hour interview, particularly if you intend to keep to time. A single, reflective, open question can work equally well in this situation.

Working with parents to generate research questions

Exploratory projects are often features of the second or third cycle of action research. Previous exploration has thrown up a series of questions, some of them the 'bigger' questions, like *'Why do Year 10s suddenly become unwilling to accept public praise?'* or *'How much do we need to know about how children have slept and eaten in order to assess how ready they are to learn in the morning?'* Teachers may have reached a point where they are unsure which is the 'right', or indeed the most relevant, research question. Schools may wish to engage in consultation about their strengths and weaknesses with parents as part of self-evaluation and the quest for continuous improvement.

For any and all of these reasons, exploratory research projects arise. There are two key elements: getting a broad spectrum of opinion and getting an in-depth under-standing of those opinions. These are potentially in conflict, so it is important to get a feedback cycle built into the design from the start. For example, an exploratory research project might start with the report of a successful Ofsted inspection. The report is circulated to all parents, together with a letter which draws their attention to the section on areas for improvement and asks for general comments and suggestions as to how the school should approach them. By far the largest number of comments come from parents interested in the way in which the school can improve its out of hours study support through the website, so the enquiry focus for the school is how to improve both the content and the uptake of the website. However, the school is concerned to keep all parents informed and on-side, so they send a letter home with a tear-off response sheet (see Box 5.3).

Box 5.3

A letter to parents

Thank you for your responses to our good Ofsted report, a credit to our staff and students. Most people have responded to the areas for improvement by saying that they'd like us to focus on the study support part of our website. We'll be working on all the areas highlighted by the inspectors but we'd like to know your top priorities, too. Please put '1' next to the most important and so on, down to '6' for the least important.

Lunchtime clubs	Study support on the website
Changing facilities in the gym	Mentor programme for Year 7s
Extended hours in the library and ICT areas	School garden

Potentially, they have missed a trick by not putting this sheet in with the Ofsted report itself but the reality is that you rarely think of these things at the time and they get a reasonable response rate of around 40%, which confirms that the website is the top priority, though changing rooms in the gym and extended hours for the library also score highly. Taking this into account, the research question begins to change, becoming about independent study and access to resources. The school designs a questionnaire for pupils about homework and independent study which asks about resources at home and the workload across the week in different subjects – this is filled in during Form group time and has a 98% response rate – and the analysis reveals that there are particular resource 'flashpoints' especially relating to GCSE coursework and resources. These results are shared with the parents through paper letters and the new parent webmail service, which sends emails to parents tailored to their child/ren's year group(s) and special interests. The letter asks for parent volunteers from the sixth form to come in to a series of subject-specific focus groups discussing their experiences of coursework, and for volunteers from the GCSE years to become part of an advisory group to develop better resources.

Parents from years 7 and 8 are invited to a series of open events in the day and evening to explore the current website and library provision alongside teaching assistants.

The school reports and open evenings in this school year have explicit feedback sheets and opportunities to informally canvass parents' opinions about the changes and the current provision. It becomes clear that there is a core group of active parents who have become very involved in the project and a larger group who are interested but who feel they cannot offer time or expertise. Of particular concern is a smaller group who feel that their resources do not stretch to providing ICT at home and who are becoming increasingly worried that this is significantly disadvantaging their children.

At each stage, the project team within the school feed back information to the parents and this builds up parents' confidence that they have a voice. The extension of library and ICT hours to include Saturday morning access became a higher priority as a result of the open evening data and funding was diverted to provide staffing. A mini-project to track the 'extended hours users' was initiated, with early self-report from students and homework feedback suggesting that it was of significant value.

Keeping your balance: consultation, collaboration and partnership

Earlier in this chapter we talked about the various approaches to research involving parents as if they were separate, or necessarily stages in a linear process. Of course, over time, they begin to form themselves into an overlapping figure (see Figure 5.4) where the findings from one kind of enquiry inform another, reflecting different priorities at different times in the research cycle.

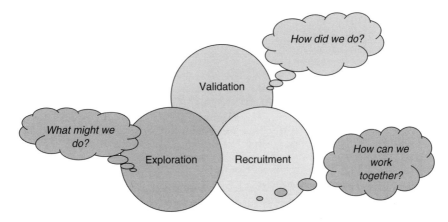

Figure 5.4   Research approaches with parents can overlap

It is very difficult for teachers to balance the competing demands of students' immediate needs, curriculum change, assessment regimes and personal and professional development. Sometimes, working with parents can seem to be an additional demand on an already over-burdened profession: an area of risk (since few teachers have been trained to work with parents) and scant reward (since the development of effective home–school partnerships takes time. The need for close relationships to sustain home–school links is made harder by the reality that school populations are transient; the effort needs to be made anew with each cohort of students. Parent involvement is never 'sorted' and this can be a source of frustration for teachers and for schools.

Engaging with parents through enquiry, however, provides a joint task with an explicit outcome that aims to benefit students. This is motivation for teachers and parents alike and there are many attendant benefits from joint endeavour: the development of a shared language about learning; opportunities to discuss the priorities for students' learning and a sense that the learning experience can be tailored to meet the needs of the students currently in the classroom. Having a short-term goal like this is far more achievable than a vague desire to 'work more closely' or 'encourage parents to become more engaged', though it is possible to move towards both of those worthy aspirations.

Key perspectives on working with parents

While parental involvement continues to be an area of concern, discussion and engagement, there are multiple perspectives on the ways in which schools and parents can, do and should interact.

Crozier, G. and Reay, D. (2005) *Activating Participation: Parents and Teachers Working Towards Partnership*. Stoke on Trent: Trentham Books.

Gewirtz, S., Ball, S. J. and Bowe, R. (1995) *Markets, Choice and Equity in Education*. Buckingham: Open University Press.

Todd, L. (2006) *Partnerships for Inclusive Education: A Critical Approach to Collaborative Working*. London: Routledge.

Wolfendale, S. (1992) *Empowering Parents and Teachers: Working for Children*. London: Cassell.

References used in this chapter

Desforges, C. and Abouchaar, A. (2003) *The Impact of Parental Involvement, Parental Support and Family Education on Pupil Achievements and Adjustment: A Literature Review*. London: Department for Education and Skills.

Hall, E. and Santer, J. (2001) 'Building relationships with parents: lessons in time and space from three research projects', in C. Day and D. van Veen (eds) *Educational Research in Europe Yearbook 2000*. Leuven: Garant.

Harding, N. (2006) 'Ethnic and social class similarities and differences in mothers' beliefs about kindergarten preparation', *Race, Ethnicity and Education,* 9(2): 223–37.

HEFCE (2005) *Young Participation in Higher Education.* Available for download from http://www.hefce.ac.uk/pubs/hefce/2005/05_03/

Mirza, H. S. (2006) '"Race", gender and educational desire', *Race, Ethnicity and Education,* 9(2): 137–58.

Sacker, A., Schoon, I., and Bartley, M. (2002) 'Social inequality in educational achievement and psychological adjustment throughout childhood: magnitude and mechanisms', *Social Science and Medicine,* 22(5): 863–80.

6

Making Sense of Your Evidence and Bringing it all Together

CHAPTER CONTENTS

- Authenticity often means a degree of 'measures' when carrying out a teacher enquiry
- It is important to explore the process of the enquiry as well as discussing the outcomes
- Communicating the experience of carrying out the enquiry is an important contribution to the replicability of the study
- Be rigorous about the kinds of claims that you can make from the analysis of your data
- Suggestions for what to include in a written report of your study.

Introduction: the experience of research – flexibility and messiness

We have structured this book as if research were a fairly linear process, since a book that reflected the unpredictability of real life research would be difficult to read. However, we want to emphasise that research projects, however well planned, are messy entities: timescales slip, personnel change and research tools seldom elicit exactly the answers we intend. Often, unexpected findings, problems and new questions emerge out of the process of enquiry, not just in the period of reflection at the end of the cycle but during data collection.

The reality of work in schools and the additional commitment that an enquiry brings means that you may well be collecting data over a fairly extended period and it is likely that you will be analysing some portions of data while you are still collecting other sources. This can be an advantage, since you will have the flexibility to collect additional information if something has not gone to plan or if the research tool you used didn't answer your question in the way you'd anticipated. It is important to accept a level of messiness in research so that you can continue your project but there is a balance to be struck: if the burning question that emerges during data collection will entail a significant additional effort – new methods, new data collection, lots more time – then it may be wiser to postpone answering that question until the next enquiry cycle.

Having accepted this potential messiness, there will come a point when you feel that you have collected all or most of your data and you will be mainly focused on analysis and the dissemination of the findings. This chapter will go through this process, exploring how to approach different types of data and deciding on analysis techniques.

It is important, however, at this stage before embracing the final stages of the research cycle to take some time to reflect on the process of the research, as well as the content of the results. The experience of research, drawn from your memory or your research diary is a vital part of your findings and the following key questions will help you to explore your action research process:

- What went according to plan?
- What was easier?
- What was more difficult?
- What had you predicted?
- What surprised you?
- What other things would you tell someone?

We have talked (in Chapters 1 and 2) about rigour in research and one of the crucial elements of rigour is replicability: can someone else read or hear about your work and then go on to do a similar kind of study in their own setting? It is vital that you give details of the way in which you have worked (including the successes and failures), who you have worked with and the measures that you have used to gauge change. It is important that you communicate the experience to those who follow as well as the results of your research, they are arguably equally important.

What have you got?

To assess where you are and what you need to do next, it is useful if you can create a record of your data collection similar to that of Table 6.1. This is invaluable while you are writing up to remind you of how many questionnaires, how long a gap between pre- and post-tests and whether all your interviews came after the observations, or if there was some overlap. This table can be used to tell the story of your data collection.

It is also useful at this point to think about the successes and failures which chart any research project: how well did each of the research methods work? Did they measure what you expected/hoped? In other words you need to think about the reliability and validity of each of the methods, to what extent will the data collection tools collect the same data and produce the same findings over time and to what extent do your tools measure what you intended. So for example with

Table 6.1 Record of Data Collection

Kind of data	Details (number of participants, tools used)	Number of collections (dates)
School data: attendance behaviour		
Attainment data		
Observations		
Questionnaires		
Interviews		
Audio/video		
Other (including research diaries)		

school data such as attendance data and SATs tests, you would expect that they would be very good in measuring the same thing over time (have high reliability) and yet unless your research question is explicitly about pupil attendance or attainment in tests then the validity might be lower. In another scenario, interviews with a group of pupils are likely to be high in validity, in that you are likely to target questions which have a high association with your research questions; however in that the group of pupils is unlikely to stay the same (they will get older or they will be replaced by a new class) then the reliability is lower. This should not mean that you discard any of your evidence, particularly where you have triangulated data collection tools thus increasing validity, but it does mean that you can prioritise your thinking about the different sets of results.

Approaching the analysis

The sections that follow in this chapter will address some of the different techniques and considerations that different kinds of data require. There are, however, key principles when analysing which apply to all kinds of data.

You are trying to answer your key research questions

The enquiry process will have thrown up all kinds of new ideas and themes, but it is important not to get sidetracked. As you work through your data, have your question pinned up somewhere prominent to help you keep focused. Look for evidence that confirms or refutes your hypothesis, and put everything else in the 'interesting but not for now' pile.

Keep an analysis log

Write down every question that you ask the data in your research diary as you go along. This seems time-consuming in the short term but it is nothing to having to re-analyse all your interviews because you can't remember if you searched for a particular theme, or re-watching all your videos looking for the interactions of a particular child. The analysis log is also a record of your developing thinking and is very useful in structuring your writing up.

Follow your hunches about themes

As you work through the data, you will start to get a sense of what is important in your project: ideas and evidence will start to form clusters. At first, they might not seem to amount to much but bear in mind that you know more about this enquiry than anyone and your hunches are likely to be based on evidence that you have noticed in passing. This is the time to examine your hunches: note them in your diary and start to record evidence under the headings you've generated. You can search for common words and phrases which relate to these themes and explore whether different kinds of evidence come together under headings (do your test results and your interviews both support the theme?) and so begin to build a picture of where your evidence is strong.

Be careful about finding what you're looking for

It is inevitable that an enquiry that looks for a particular change will find *some* evidence of that change. It is human nature to seize on the positive evidence and place it 'front and centre' in a research report and to give a less prominent position to the ambiguous or negative findings. It is therefore incredibly important to do lots of counting, especially in qualitative research. If you have two wonderful quotes from interviews supporting your argument in the write-up, they will be even more wonderful if you can report that they are representative of the twenty-five positive statements given on this theme and that only four negative statements were made. The reader will not suspect that you have just cherry-picked those two and ignored the rest.

Your conclusions will be stronger if you can validate them

Working collaboratively with colleagues and research participants is the best way to ensure that your interpretation of the data is reasonable and representative. There are a variety of ways that you can approach this: you can ask a colleague to watch a short piece of video or read part of an interview transcript, without telling him what your conclusions have been and simply ask him what seems to be interesting or important. You can feed back your analysis at an early stage to research participants, by reporting questionnaire results to parents or students and asking them to flesh out the headlines, or to challenge your assumptions. As a matter of good practice, anything you write about others should be available to them for their comment at a draft stage. Not everyone will want to read or comment on your research but the opportunity to pick up on errors of fact or interpretation should be there. Your research conclusions will be so much stronger when backed up by the validation of your colleagues and your participants.

School data

You may well have made use of the masses of data relating to attendance and behaviour that schools collect every day. You need to be clear about what the data is: if you are looking at behaviour monitoring data for a group of students you need to state what is being recorded, by whom and when. You need to decide if it is a fair comparison to look at behaviour referrals from different staff members – does everyone use the same criteria? If you are confident that they do, you can report and compare levels of referral without further comment. However, if you are not sure, you will need to report that these are possible indications of students' behaviour. At the first level, you need to do counts and to keep accurate records of the time-frame, you can then go on to do comparisons with other groups or other years. Depending on the data, you may be able to make statements about cohorts, classes or individuals. The level of analysis and reporting that you use is up to you and is dependent on your audience: the example below gives a description of the measurement used and several different approaches to analysis.

Example

In order to judge the effectiveness of the project we looked at the numbers of students signed into the Late Book. Only students who are more than 15 minutes late (i.e., arriving after 9am) sign the book, since at that time the only point of entrance is the main foyer and they sign the book on their way in.

Descriptive

During the project, 24 students were signed into the late book, fewer than we would normally expect.

Comparative

In the spring term of 2006, 48 students signed in late, whereas in spring 2007 only 24 signed in late.

Analytic

During the 'Don't Be Late' project, the number of children signing in late fell by 50% compared to the previous year (n = 24 in 2007, 48 in 2006). The latecomers were boys more than girls (17/7 in 2007, 31/17 in 2006) and were more likely to be older.

Analytic (individual tracking)

During the 'Don't Be Late' project, the number of children signing in late fell by 50% compared to the previous year (n = 24 in 2007, 48 in 2006).

The latecomers were more boys than girls (17/7 in 2007, 31/17 in 2006) and were more likely to be older. Of those children signing in late in 2007, the majority (n = 16) were from Years 10 and 11 and only one was from Year 7. With the exception of this Year 7 student, all the students signing in late in 2007 had been late in 2006.

Attainment data

When looking at attainment data it is hard not to get sucked into the sort of mindset which suggests that only a significant improvement in nationally standardised tests 'counts'. Within research, however, a range of measures are commonly used: teacher assessments, standardised tests and national assessments measure different outcomes. Some assessment measures require you to perform both pre- and post-tests, while others are 'norm-referenced' and allow you to use them once and then compare the results to scores matched to average performance by age. This is where your research question and your intent in the enquiry are crucial: you need to be clear about whether the kind of question you asked matches the measure you've used, and this affects the kinds of comparative statements you can make (see Table 6.2 for some examples).

Table 6.2   Ways of Reporting Performance Data

Question	Measure	Comparison
How well can Jimmy do on Task A? (standardised)	Norm-referenced test of performance on Task A	Jimmy's score is above average for his age
Can Jimmy get better at Task A? (ipsative 1)	Pre- and post-test designed to measure performance on Task A	Jimmy improved his pre-test score by 10 points
Can Jimmy get better at Task A? (ipsative 2)	Ongoing teacher assessment	Jimmy's work shows development and improvement over time
Can performance in Task A be improved in this class? (cohort 1)	National test data (e.g., SATs, GCSEs)	Jimmy's class have scored higher than last year's group
Can performance in Task A be improved in this class? (cohort 2)	Pre- and post-test designed to measure performance on Task A	Jimmy's class have all improved their scores by between 3 and 14 points

You'll notice that none of the examples in Table 6.2 use a contemporary control group — a matched group sitting the same assessment at the same time. Control groups are used less frequently in practitioner enquiry and some teachers feel that this makes their research less valid. We would argue that the question is not one of validity but of the kinds of claims you can make for the data: you can't use any of that data to make a direct causal link between the score Jimmy achieved and the intervention used by his teacher to effect change. You can speculate that the difference between pre- and post-testing might be connected to the intervention and you could also speculate that the difference between this cohort and the previous one was affected by the changes the teacher made, but you would need much more information about how similar that cohort was to Jimmy's class before you could make that claim with confidence. However, supposing that Jimmy's teacher was able to persuade her colleague in Year 6, who had a class from broadly similar backgrounds, with the same mix of ability levels, first language and other relevant factor to run pre- and post-tests of critical thinking with her students, without employing the critical thinking curriculum. This looks like a workable control group and differences between the scores can be looked at (see Table 6.3).

Table 6.3 Example of Reporting Experimental and Control Group Data

	Number of students	Pre-test scores Average (range)	Post-test scores Average (range)
Jimmy's class	30	21 (13–32)	29 (17–44)
Control class	29	16 (11–24)	19 (13–29)

The obvious first implications of this data are that Jimmy's teacher has proved her hypothesis: a critical thinking intervention has shifted all her students' scores up — though the range suggests that the effect is variable and some children got more from it than others — and her class has done significantly better in the post-test than the control group, suggesting that they have done much better than they would have done without the intervention. However, it's important to look closely at the control group scores to make sure that we don't over-state the effect that Jimmy's teacher has had. The control group class score lower on the pre-test, too, suggesting that Jimmy's teacher has been infusing critical thinking skills in her teaching already (there's a reason she chose this intervention — it suits her beliefs and the way she likes to work with the children). Moreover, the control class makes some progress over time, between 2 and 5 points at the top and bottom of the range (and you'd have to check for individual children in that group making greater leaps, or even going backwards, averages can hide a lot), so you'd have to subtract a small amount from the gains that Jimmy's class made to account for this. The reason for all this caution is the way in which research findings can be used: if you look at the headlines of this research, you might conclude that all the teachers in Jimmy's school should use the critical thinking intervention and that it would have a broadly equivalent effect on all the children. Our experience in the real world of learning and teaching suggests that this is not the case.

Observations, including audio and video

When you do an observation, you are analysing from the moment you begin. Before you even pick up a pencil, you have decided upon what to record, and what to ignore. The inherent slant in an observation makes the counting part of the analysis all the more important. Tally charts are a good place to start, based around the following questions: *who, what, when, with whom, how many, how often, how long* and as many others as you need to address your question.

Example

Moira was observing the use of the role play area as part of her enquiry into children's use of mathematical language in their play. These tally charts represent data from two periods of observations at each end of her project.

Who/How many	Early observations	Later observations
Anna	2	3
Ben	0	1
Charlie	4	3
Dawn	0	0
Eddie	3	5
Farah	2	2

With whom	Early observations	Later observations
Anna	Saira, Nadia	Saira, Helen
Ben		Eddie
Charlie	Nick	Nick
Eddie	Tyrone, Josh, Philip	Ben, Tyrone, Farah
Farah	Lucy, Josh	Eddie, Nadia

What/who	Early observations	Later observations
House (chores)	Saira, Nadia	
House (relationships)	Farah, Lucy	Saira, Helen
Fantasy (task/ adventure)	Tyrone, Josh, Philip, Lucy, Charlie, Nick	Ben, Tyrone, Farah, Charlie, Charlie, Nick Nick
Fantasy (relationships)	Anna, Saira	Anna, Helen

Often with observations, you will be comparing over time and one critical element here is to make sure that the description of the behaviour observed is accurate. This is important even when you are doing all the observations, as your focus may shift over time, but it is crucial if the observations are being done by others as well as you. Many hours spent in meetings debating what is meant by an open question or what constitutes off-task behaviour have convinced us that it is well worth having this clarified early, written down and adhered to. From your research diary, you will need to make clear how similar the occasions of repeat observations were to the first, what the differences were and what impact you judge these differences to have made, if any.

Once you have made the counts, you can explore the patterns which are emerging, some of which may be surprising. By basing your analysis of themes on the counts, you will be able to report accurately whether an observed incident is typical, part of a larger pattern of behaviour for a group or individual or unusual, yet significant. It is very important to distinguish between an observed behaviour which is typical of the other behaviours in your observations and one which only occurs infrequently in the observation but which you have often experienced in 'normal' classroom life. Your ongoing experience with the students is data, but it is a different kind of data and must be reported differently from a structured observation.

For audio and video recordings, you need to follow a similar protocol with regard to counting, though by using these technologies, things like length of speech and non-verbal interactions become easier to explore. Video and audio are very data rich, so choose short sections to analyse for your own sanity but be very clear to report if these are typical or unusual excerpts. Of course, permission is required from staff, pupils and parents to use visual images in reporting (see Chapter 4). Observations are particularly prone to interpretation by the observer, so a discussion with 'the observed' to validate your analysis is particularly helpful here. If you have used audio or video, you can play short sections and describe your interpretation, giving colleagues or students an opportunity to support or challenge your understanding.

Questionnaires

If you have used questionnaires the first task, which you can get started with before you get any back, is constructing your database. The best place to do this is in Excel, since it is easier to use than other statistical packages and has the facility to make graphs quickly and effectively. Using the first page of the questionnaire from Chapter 5 devised by Lanner School in Cornwall, a fictitious sample of results is given in Table 6.4.

Lanner Parent Questionnaire

About your child's learning at school

1 How confident are you that you know **what** your child is learning at school? *Please tick one box*

Not at all confident	I know some of what is going on	I know most of what is going on	Very confident

2 How do you find out what your child is learning at school? Please tick all that apply

The school send me letters and leaflets	My child tells me	My child's teacher tells me	I hear about things from other parents	Other (*please state below*)

Other ways of finding out _____

3 How confident are you that you understand **how** your child is learning at school? *Please tick one box*

Not at all confident	I know some of what is going on	I know most of what is going on	Very confident

4 How do you find out **how** your child is learning at school? *Please tick all that apply*

The school send me letters and leaflets	My child tells me	My child's teacher tells me	I hear about things from other parents	Other (*please state below*)

Other ways of finding out _____

5 Would you be interested in finding out more about what and how your child is learning at school? *Please tick one box*

Yes	No

Responses are scored:

- 1–4 for Q1 and Q3
- 1–5 for Q2 and Q4
- for Q5, Yes scores 1, No scores 0.

The teachers at Lanner asked a range of open and closed questions, so there are a variety of things that can be done with this data. For questions 1 and 3 there are some simple calculations that can be performed: by adding up the totals one can see that parents in this sample are more confident about *what* their children are learning than about *how* they are learning it. Calculating the mean and standard deviation focuses attention on those few parents at the extremes of confidence both high and low as atypical. Questions 2 and 4 ask for the source of information, which can be represented in another table (see Table 6.5), where it becomes clear that children themselves are the main source of information on the process of learning.

At this point it becomes tempting to speculate: are there connections between where you get your information and how confident you are?; does the level of confidence impact on desire to get involved?; do other parents make you feel more or less confident? Some, though by no means all, of these questions are addressed by this data and speculative questions like these should be reported as 'areas for further investigation'.

Table 6.4   Results of Lanner Parent Questionnaire

	Q1	Q2	Q2 Other	Q3	Q4	Q4 Other	Q5
Parent 1	3	1, 2, 4		2	2		1
Parent 2	3	2, 3		3	2, 3		1
Parent 3	2	2, 4		2	2, 4		1
Parent 4	1	5	No-one tells me	1	5	I don't know who to ask	1
Parent 5	4	1, 3		4	1, 2, 3		0
Parent 6	2	1, 2		1	2		1
Parent 7	3	1, 2, 3		3	2, 3		1
Parent 8	2	1, 4		1	2, 4		1
Parent 9	1	2, 4		1	2		0
Parent 10	4	1, 2		3	2, 3		1
Total	25			21			8
Mean	2.5			2.1			
S.D	1.08			1.1			

Table 6.5   Sources of Information

	School	Child	Teacher	Parents	Other
Information on what	6	5	3	4	1
Information on how	1	9	4	2	1

Interviews

Interviews are at the same time the hardest and the most pleasurable things to analyse because they are so rich and contain so much for you to engage with. Even using a very structured schedule, there will be all kinds of surprising and interesting themes which can emerge. So, back to your key research questions in order to keep on track. The transcript below is a section from a much longer interview with a teacher about his research. The annotations represent the first level notes made in the analysis of this and the other interviews in this series, highlighting sections which relate to the principle object of the interviews – exploring research-active teachers' influence on their colleagues - noting key phrases and words which will be searched for throughout the data set. In addition, a particular phrase is highlighted. When I heard the words during the interview I became quite excited; this was exactly what we were looking for! It would even make a rather good journal article title. This is the 'seductive quote': the answer to a researcher's prayer and more frequently than we'd like, our downfall. It is too easy to be dazzled by quotes like this and to give them undue prominence in your writing. Unfortunately for my phantom article, not enough of the other data from the interviews supported this to make it a fully-fledged theme.

Elaine: Could you start with what you feel the most important changes have been as a result of this project?

Bob: I think that the most important change is probably been getting the whole school learning rather than teaching. Is that sufficient or would you like me to go further?

Sections relevant to our research question 'How do teachers engaged in research influence their colleagues?'

Elaine: Yes please that sounds really interesting.

Bob: Well it's there are lots of other things that I am trying to do at the moment, not least the KS 3 strategy and that kind of thing, which has come on the back of the research project work. The [funding body] started as a major influence in all of that. Me taking on research projects in the school has made my colleagues really **reflect** on why they are doing what they are doing and why we're doing what we are doing as a school. I did a thing about the research, a whole staff inset evening about 3 months ago. I got some tremendous **feedback** from that, that made me understand what an impact it had. In my jaundiced moments I think 'why am I doing this, why am I doing this?' but actually the **feedback** was fantastic and a lot of people saw the research project if nothing else acting as a '**conscience for the school**'. It is a phrase that I coined but other people bought into it, this idea that we otherwise bundle along doing stuff and not **reflecting** on why we are doing it.

Key words from the project to search for in this interview (and others)
  Reflect (ing/ion)
  Feedback

'Conscience for the school', fantastic quote!! (Beware …)

As you read and re-read your interviews (or listen and re-listen to audio recordings if you haven't transcribed them) you'll become aware of frequencies and trends in your data and will be able to build up themes, gathering together quotes and sections. However you do this, by cutting and pasting in Word, or snipping up copies of the interviews and putting them in folders, you must keep a record of how many individuals support a theme and how many times they support it. Bob's interview contains a great deal of material on the importance of staff meetings for the development of research culture but the seven quotes from him are not enough to emphasise this factor in the research report without the evidence that nine other teachers talked about it in their interviews as well. In reporting interview data you must say how many people mention something that you advance as evidence and how often: '*A lot of students were positive about the project*' is not nearly as strong as '*Seven out of the eight students interviewed had positive things to say about the project. Commonly used terms were "exciting" (n = 6), "fun" (n = 12) and "challenging" (n = 5). The negative comments from the other student also related to challenge: "I thought the whole thing was too hard for us, it felt like it had been designed for older kids."*'

As this example indicates, it is a good idea to highlight the contrasts in your data, the elements which challenge the majority view and your hypothesis. When asking people to be interviewed you offer them a platform to express their views, so you are ethically obliged to represent their views, even if you give greater weight to the views of others. So much of the analysis of interviews depends on your judgement, so it is important to validate your themes and to weave together the data from your interviews with data from other sources, such as observations and school or assessment data.

Structuring your report

When you are thinking about the information to include in a report about your enquiry it is useful to contemplate one of three frames which can help to structure the process. Firstly, it is useful to think of the things you as a teacher would need to know to persuade you to use a specific innovation in your own teaching: the school/classroom context, the demographics of the class, the organisation decisions that needed to be made, the preparation involved and an honest appraisal of the successes and failures. In that you are likely to have an audience of teachers, then it is important to keep their agendas in mind.

The second frame we would recommend is a structure that should be familiar as one recommended in Science from Key Stage 2 upwards, the experiment write up: what you wanted to find out, what you did, how you did it, what your findings were and what this means to you. This structure will extend what could be a lesson plan into the genre of research study, an investigation.

The third frame, and arguably the most important, is the action research frame: it is important to remember that your report is part of a process; you are at the 'making it public stage' of one cycle, but you will be quickly moving forward into the next cycle of enquiry. This means there needs to be an aspect of your write up which looks forward, appraising the lessons learnt about teaching processes and research methods and the implications for school, teachers, pupils and parents, but also the implications for your own research focus – where will you be heading next: what is the next hunch you would like to explore and what are the links and learning which has got you there? The latter element is particularly important if findings have not been what you hoped or expected, there can still be some positive learning which can be achieved and the research can move on to address the issues. This can be seen in the quote below:

> In Year One of the research our findings were extremely positive with a positive effect size of 0.76 for peer assessment of writing; in other words an average class using this approach would move up from 50th to 23rd in a ranked list of 100 classes. However, in the second year of the research the findings were not as positive and although we learned from the conclusions and the school was able to move forward, the actual writing up was difficult in that we did not feel we had much positive to say.

Included in the box below are some of the headings used by teachers in the Learning to Learn Phase 3 Evaluation to support the writing up process. In this project the teachers completed a written report which was available for download on the Campaign for Learning's website. This meant the audience was very open and the report had to try to be all things to all people. Hopefully there are elements from all three frames above apparent in the headings. We do not advocate that you need to use all or any of these specific headings, but it should provide a useful starting point from which you can devise your own structure. Under each of the headings on the next page, there is also some guidance as to what could be included under each section. As before this is meant as a starting point and is by no means meant as a definitive list.

Context

The school:
Year groups involved
Details of school catchment
Statistics such as school roll, % SEN, % EAL and % FSM
How involved in the project
Background of school in relation to educational research Achievement

The teacher(s):
Background in school and in teaching, including relevant interests and research

The Project:

Rationale:
Reasons for involvement in project Why this area
Need of the pupils
Relate to interests and background

Objectives:
Subject area
Key objectives
Target pupils

(Continued)

Curriculum and
development interests
Influences
Interest in project: benefits
and challenges

The pupils:
Focus Year group/class and
why
Number in class/year group
% SEN etc
Characteristics e.g., lively,
inquisitive
Targets and achievements
while in school

Discussion of Results:

Findings:
Whether your findings have
achieved your initial aims
Evidence in support of and
against your hypothesis
Interesting aspects of the
process

Unexpected effects
Benefits to pupils
Benefits for the teacher(s)
Negative effects for
teacher(s) and pupils
Evidence from
pupil/teacher/parent quotes
can be included here
Evidence in the form of
digital images can also be
included here

**Extensions and changes to
method:**

Did you change anything
while the project
progressed?
Why?
What were the effects of this?

Hypothesis:
Written in the form of a
question

Research Process:

Teachers' choices:
How the teacher(s) chose to
tackle the project aims
Which strategies were
chosen and why
Detail about how the
strategies were implemented
in the classroom
Reaction towards the
research process and the
choice of method

Evidence collected:
Data collected to record
whether aims achieved
Reasons for choosing
different methods of data
collection

Conclusions:

Developing this approach:
If you used this process again
what would you keep the
same?
What would you make
different?
Why?
Any adaptations to the
strategies used?
How would it work on a
larger scale?
How would it work with other
age ranges?
Changes to strategies used
School developments as a
consequence
Teacher developments as a
consequence

What did you do extra?
Why?
Influence on the project

Pupil developments as a
consequence

Summary:
3 most important
impacts/findings of the
project
How the teacher(s) felt
about the project as a whole
Impact on school
Impact on teacher
Impact on pupils

Sharing Your Findings

CHAPTER CONTENTS

- Sharing findings and learning from your research
- Matching the dissemination of your findings with your intentions and your audience
- Making links with existing research
- The impact of action research on professional development and school improvement
- Engaging in debate with the wider professional and academic community.

Teacher-researchers need to present their findings – this is a priority.

(Teacher-researcher, Leading Edge Action Research Partnership School)

Sharing findings and learning from your research

In the first instance, sharing your findings is important because it helps you to articulate and clarify your thoughts making it a crucial part of learning from the research. The teachers we have worked with comment on how discussion of their findings leads them to realise new things about routine behaviour in the classroom:

> … we had never really discussed why we record in different ways. We had never reflected on why on some days we do not do any recording … This made us stop and think. (Y3 L2L Case Study, Kehelland School)

Sometimes teachers are reluctant to share their findings because they lack confidence in the status and credibility of their research as it seems small in scale or too closely linked to their own concerns. Whilst it may not always be possible to present this new learning in a polished form, it is significant and charting the move from a belief or a 'hunch' about an issue to collecting evidence and formulating an interpretation of the outcome is vital. The process of enquiry and reflection is an important part of dealing with the messy and ill-structured problems we face in the daily practice of the classroom; it is because teacher research is specific to a particular context and deals with complexity that it is so valuable. It is also important for colleagues not directly involved to hear about what you have been doing. Your findings can contribute to the promotion of professional dialogue within your school by posing problems, highlighting issues and outlining possible solutions based on real situations. It is accounts from people who have direct experience of teaching and learning in classrooms that can be the most persuasive:

> Authentic stories of learning and leadership need to be told through the voice of those who lived the stories. (Krovetz and Arriaza, 2006)

Sharing your findings is also part of the process of translating learning from one context to another which can have an impact on the wider educational community and challenge the usual division between theory and practice (Ball and Cohen, 1999). Lawrence Stenhouse saw teacher enquiry as offering a new perspective on research:

> ... it is not enough that teachers' work should be studied: they need to study it for themselves. What we need is a different view of research which begins with our own work and which is founded in curiosity and a desire to understand; which is stable, not fleeting, systematic in the sense of being sustained by a strategy. (Stenhouse, 1995: 1)

Developments in understanding the importance of situated learning and knowledge creation through participation in a community of practice (Lave and Wenger, 1991) are also useful in working towards this new model for research which aims to strengthen professional judgement.

Whilst sharing your findings may be important for your own professional learning, your colleagues and the wider educational community, it can still be a challenging process:

> Overall we have found the research useful, but the difficulty of making public and personally dealing with, after a great deal of hard work, neutral or negative findings should not be underestimated.   (Y3 Case Study, Wilbury School)

John Dewey, an advocate of the value of teacher enquiry, talked of the need for 'critical optimism' (Shields, 2003) in order to manage the uncertainty and disappointment that can occur. It is important to be working within an environment where problem–posing as well as problem-solving is valued and in which encouragement to experiment also recognises that not everything will necessarily succeed. Another issue is the role of writing in the sharing of findings, with some people seeing it as an essential component (Kelly, 2006), whereas for others it is adding another burden to an already heavy workload. In the next section we consider different ways of disseminating your findings and matching these with your intentions and your audience.

Matching the dissemination of your findings with your intentions and your audience

The teachers with whom we have worked have used a variety of ways of sharing their findings including:

- Notice-boards around the school

Information about a project and any findings can be shared by having a designated notice-board in the staffroom or in the school entrance on which photographs, examples of any tools used, pupils' work and brief summaries of the evidence are displayed.

- Show and tell lunches

The senior management provide a small budget to pay for a free lunch once a month and teachers take turns to present what they are doing and share ideas with colleagues.

- Presentations in school assemblies

This can be very effective when pupils take the lead in describing what has been happening and the impact it has had on their learning. In primary schools it can also be a way of letting parents know what is happening and what you are finding out.

- Regular items in staff briefings and bulletins
- CPD conferences and joint training days with teacher (and student) researchers leading workshops

The schools which have used teachers and pupils to present workshops on training days frequently report that the evaluations show that staff rate these as highly effective forms of CPD.

- Adding a teaching and learning section to the staff handbook using short summaries of projects written by teacher researchers
- Website links to ongoing research activity in the school

Putting a section on research with tools and examples of projects can be useful but this usually needs to be linked to other methods of sharing findings as people tend not to use websites without prompting unless they are built into their daily life.

- Creation of Lead Learner posts within school

Some schools are using the Advanced Skills Teacher (AST) role to embed a research culture in their schools by including responsibility for promoting research in the job description.

- Peer observation and coaching

Structures are in place in some schools which enable staff to participate in a programme of peer observation and coaching after which they evaluate the impact of what they have observed on the development of teaching and learning in their own classes. Time is given to staff to do the observations and write up the evaluation and the reports are seen as a valuable data source. It is important to maintain a distinction between this kind of collaborative working and any existing structures linked to performance management.

- Making small grants or sabbatical time available for staff with interesting project proposals which include building on the work of existing research in school
- Learning walks

This is based on the idea developed by the National College for School Leadership as part of their Networked Learning Communities initiative. Exchange visits by staff from schools are organised in which a project is described and then participants are invited to walk around the school, visit classrooms and look for evidence of the impact of the work. In some cases the host school identifies what the focus during the walk should be and in others it is the visitors who do this; at the end of the walk different impressions and perspectives are shared in an informal discussion. Some of the most successful Learning Walks have been those which involved pupils visiting each other's schools and comparing pupil and teacher views of learning in different contexts has itself led to a new focus for enquiry.

Within the variety of ways of sharing findings that schools are developing, common characteristics can be identified:

- Production of practical, tangible artefacts

This is consistent with what has been highlighted as important for communities of practice where learning is situated. The use of practical tools can structure participation and further understanding (Bielaczyc and Collins, 1999). Teachers need something that they can apply and test out in their own practice and this can trigger interest in becoming involved in enquiry for themselves or willingness to learn more from colleagues. Teachers will often talk about 'stealing' good ideas from colleagues and the artefacts can be a means of building on this tendency to promote the dissemination of research within a school.

- Aim for transparency so that the process, as well as any outcomes, is shared

We have already emphasised the importance of making any reporting of an enquiry transparent as part of the means of ensuring the rigour of your research. Colleagues also need to know how any tools have been developed and used in order to have the capacity to make best use of them and adapt and innovate.

- Encourage replication

Presenting your findings in forms that can be used but which also make the processes of their production and use clear, invites colleagues to replicate what you have done. By applying the outcomes of your enquiry in a new context they will be able to either validate them or pose new questions (often they will do both at the same time). The invitation is, in the spirit of collaborative enquiry, to 'try this for yourselves, this is what I did and this is what I found, what do you think?'

- Create structures of support

In our experience, the best support occurs through encouraging organic growth as is expressed succinctly by one teacher-researcher:

> Start with a small group of 'mad' people – give them the chance to feedback – show what is in it for them – show that it makes a difference – then gradually change the mindset of colleagues.

It requires the bringing together of top-down and bottom-up support so that the enthusiasts are given scope to develop their ideas within a managed system that provides encouragement, recognition and resources.

One question still remains to be answered, how important is it to have a written account of your enquiry? We have always encouraged teachers to aim for a written report of their research (see Chapter 6 for more discussion of the writing up of the report) as we think the act of writing helps to make the process of the enquiry more explicit and the report itself can be a practical, tangible artefact productive of further learning. We suggest that the requirement to write case studies is a way of developing teacher autonomy through a shared understanding of the expectations of the craft of research (Ecclestone, 2004). Other commentators on the process of teacher research also support the view that writing is an important stage in the enquiry cycle (Rickert, 1991; Somekh, 2006). However, there has recently been some discussion of what exactly it might mean for a teacher-researcher to make their enquiry public as advocated by Stenhouse. It has been suggested that it may be more appropriate in some instances to experiment with non-published forms of outcome or by publishing to the village rather than to the world (McIntyre, 2005). The reluctance of many teachers to produce formal, written outcomes from their enquiries has been noted in a number of otherwise successful teacher research projects such as the Teacher Training Agency's School-Based Research Consortia (Cordingley, Baumfield et al. 2002). The Enquiry Groups project at St Martin's College, Lancaster, has some very active teacher researchers who have decided that the process is more important than any formal, written outcome and have decided to continue with the cycles of enquiry but not produce reports (as stated at a workshop at the ESCalate conference organised by the universities of Bristol, Cumbria and Stirling in Lancaster). The requirement to produce written reports of an enquiry certainly needs to be thought about carefully, given the demands it can make on the teachers concerned and the risk of undesirable side-effects:

> ... negative effects for the teachers (and pupils) were that the school dramatically underestimated the amount of time needed to evaluate and write up the project. (Y 3 Case Study, Oakthorpe School)

It should also be recognised that producing a written account may make different kinds of demands on participants:

> ... deciding what to disclose and what to obscure or omit entails very different risks and consequences for the differently positioned writers in the group. (Cochran-Smith and Lytle, 2004: 641)

When considering the dissemination process it is worth going back to the selection of the target audience as part of your research design. In Chapter 2 this was considered in the context of a strategy for choosing data collection tools but it can also be used to focus your dissemination. You will need to think about the opportunities which are open for you to communicate about your research and which of those you think will be most suitable. What is important about the communication of any findings is that it should demonstrate fitness for purpose; in this instance that means the capacity of the outcomes from your enquiry to enable professional judgement and provide a sufficient basis, a warrant, for future action. Consequently, decisions about the method of representing what you have learned should be made according to its potential to enable participation and the application of existing skills to the solving of a problem. We know that it can be difficult to involve colleagues who have not had the experience of being part of an enquiry and this is an issue for the scaling up of any initiative within a school:

> The teachers who took on the original focus groups ... all had training in L2L and were enthusiastic about the benefits they could foresee. However, other teachers had to work out the advantages for themselves – after some persuasion from the original teachers – and, although all but one are keen and enjoying their teaching, it is a lesson to learn for the future. (Case Study report, Roseland School)

The central concern regarding the sharing of findings with a 'public' should be to support the persuasive powers of the advocates of the enquiry and to interest the wider school community. How large a part writing up the enquiry plays or what form that should take is a decision to be made in terms of your intention, audience and its fitness for purpose.

Making links with existing research

There has been some criticism of teacher research because of a tendency not to make links to existing research in the process of an enquiry and the risk that any outcomes may simply 're-invent the wheel'. On the other hand, the potential of teacher enquiry is to support the development of evidence informed practice by enhancing the relevance of existing research and building research capacity. We find that if teachers begin with investigating their own questions directly in an enquiry this will lead them at a later stage to look beyond their own experience and to take account of what other people may have said about an issue. We have described this as a process of beginning with engaging *in* research as the stimulus for engaging *with* research (Baumfield, Hall et al., 2007) so that teachers are alert to the potential of using a range of sources of information in their discussion of issues and the evaluation of new initiatives and approaches.

Promoting partnerships between schools and university researchers can facilitate the use of a wider range of sources of evidence in the process of enquiry. In Sweden there is a policy for school improvement through the combining of curriculum and teacher development through action research projects facilitated by university researchers. They have found that initially teachers relied upon individual experience rather than literature or existing research. They also found that co-operation between teachers was rare and the dissemination of ideas and results meagre. After the three-year development project working in partnership with the university, there was more teacher co-operation and dialogue in school about pedagogy leading to a desire for further knowledge (Rosendahl and Ronnerman, 2006). Making links with existing research through this kind of partnership can overcome the problem that in many cases teachers do not engage with research because, even when they are able to physically access sources (and this can be very difficult if you are not a member of academic staff or a student at a university), they find the kind of knowledge they provide does not meet their needs. Collaborative research partnerships encourage different perspectives and expertise to be employed with a shared purpose rather than, as is too often the case, reinforcing a theory and practice division that makes the translation of knowledge from one context to another very difficult:

> ... because teachers and researchers work in unconnected problem spaces – even when the problems they are working on have the same name – teachers and researchers need to work together in tackling unsolved problems that are of central importance to teaching with inquiry acting as the common driver. Modern teachers need to be simultaneously active in two knowledge building communities; with their students building an understanding of the world and with researchers and other practitioners building a working knowledge of teaching and learning. (Bereiter, 2002: 416)

Networks are important for providing mutual support:

> It gave us a sense that we were not alone in any difficulties we were hav-
> ing and it was also great to share successes and new ideas. (Teacher
> researcher, Fleecefield Primary School)

They are also important in the uptake of research evidence as building relationships and sharing the conduct and analysis of research increases confidence and
this is as important as knowing about research techniques or evidence (Simons,
Kushner et al., 2003).

The impact of action research on professional development and school improvement

> It is the belief of the author that the single most important vehicle for
> developing a teacher is the undertaking of action research. (Teacher-
> researcher, Treviglas Primary School)

Using personal experience in order to engage with a problem and construct a theory develops a critical capacity and an understanding of uncertainty that strength-
ens professional judgement (Moon 2004) and the management of change:

> … [we] look at initiatives in a different way, are more analytical about what
> will work for the child and feel open to new ways of learning and new
> methods of teaching. Trying new initiatives, trialling them, evaluating
> them and either putting them into practice or discarding them is not so
> daunting now. (Teacher-researcher, Raynham Primary School)

Enquiry and evidence-based decision making is the key to internal capacity building in schools through sustaining the continuous learning of teachers by building
on their interest in enhancing pupil learning. The gathering of concrete data in
context means that processes of review and the management of change can be
more effective. Action research can support the implementation of new ideas and
practices in school by encouraging reluctant colleagues to have a go and try new
ideas persuaded by the evidence of tangible benefits for pupils. The presence of
enthusiasts in the staffroom who are excited about what they are learning can create interest in finding out what is going on:

> … for the first time teachers were asking 'What do you and Lynn do in the
> rainbow room?' and they asked to have a staff meeting about it. (Case
> Study Report, Oakland Primary School)

Involvement in the research process gives motivation and permission to look closely at the previous methods used and trial new ways of doing things. The findings at the end of each cycle not only justify doing this but also prompt more changes to occur. Schools can develop INSET based on the outcomes of previous research findings and links have been established with annual pedagogical reviews and Self-Evaluation Forms (SEFs). Widening the circle of who is involved to include pupils as student researchers as well as parents and the local community can drive forward interlocking cycles of enquiry that enhance the research culture of the school so that intelligent questions are asked, data is interrogated and planning is evidence informed:

> The research projects are regularly shared with colleagues, pupils and parents through a variety of media and the school has a 'research culture', which lies at the heart of decision-making in school. Cross-curricular working groups both consult research projects and do their own, as policies are reviewed or created. (Case Study Report, Fallibroome Secondary School)

Researchers working in the USA who have a great deal of experience of working with teacher-researchers identify three different inquiry–knowledge–practice relationships (Cochran-Smith and Lytle, 2004):

1 Knowledge *for* practice – to implement/codify for dissemination (formal knowledge)
2 Knowledge *in* practice – to uncover and enhance (situated knowledge)
3 Knowledge *of* practice – to generate local knowledge within inquiry communities (testing knowledge in context).

Schools involved in systematic enquiry into the processes of teaching and learning foster all three forms of knowledge creation and can make a significant contribution to debate within the wider professional and academic community. Stenhouse used an analogy between aeronautical engineering and education to highlight the importance of practical, contextualised research for professional development and school improvement:

> ... to do research into building an aeroplane you have to build an aeroplane and not run along the tarmac flapping your arms – likewise, to do research into teaching you need to create some sort of instrument to research teaching. (Stenhouse 1995: 59)

He believed that parity between teachers and academics in research involving the testing of ideas through their enactment in the classroom was the way forward and this is certainly the view of the teachers with whom we have worked:

> I am intrigued with the idea of schools being research schools as many staff develop interesting teaching and learning initiatives that with some research would show how their idea is effective. (Teacher-researcher, Hazelbury Infant School)

We know that managing schools as research cultures requires careful attention to the securing of adequate support and planning for varying degrees of involvement from staff at different points in the school year and at different times in an individual's career. If development is to be sustainable then a model accommodating waves of involvement attuned to the rhythm of life in the school has been found to be effective (see Temperley and McGrane, 2005 for more detail). We also know that enquiry into practice through action research has the potential to promote professional development and make a real difference to the lives of teachers and pupils in schools. It is fitting to leave the last word on this to a pupil in one of the schools:

> You can change things if you research well enough. (Student-researcher, Leading Edge Action Research Partnership School)

References used in this chapter

Ball, D. L. and Cohen, D. K. (1999) 'Developing practice, developing practitioners: toward a practice-based theory of professional education', in D. Sykes and L. Darling-Hammond (eds), *Teaching as the Learning Profession: Handbook of Policy and Practice*. San Francisco: Jossey Bass. pp. 3–32.

Baumfield, V., Hall, E., Higgins, S. and Wall, K. (2007) 'Tools for inquiry and the role of feedback in teachers' learning'. Paper presented at the European Association of Research into Learning and Instruction (EARLI) Conference, Budapest, September 2007.

Bereiter, C. (2002) *Education and Mind in the Knowledge Age*. Mahwah, NJ: Lawrence Erlbaum Assoc.

Bielaczyc, K. and Collins, A. (1999) 'Learning communities in classrooms: a reconceptualization of educational practice', in C. M. Reigeluth (ed.), *Instructional-Design Theories and Models: A New Paradigm of Instructional Theory*. Mahwah, NJ: Lawrence Erlbaum. pp. 269–92.

Cochran-Smith, M. and Lytle, S. L. (2004) 'Practitioner inquiry, knowledge and university culture', in J. J. Loughran, M. L. Hamilton, V. K. LaBoskey and T. L. Russell (eds), *International Handbook of Self-Study of Teaching and Teacher Education Practices*. Dordrecht: Kluwer Academic Publishers.

Cordingley, P., Baumfield, V. M., Butterworth, M., McNamara, O. and Elkins, T. (2002) *Lessons from the School-based Research Consortia*. University of Exeter: British Education Research Association.

Ecclestone, K. (2004) 'Learning in a comfort zone: cultural and social capital inside an outcome-based assessment regime', *Assessment in Education: Principles, Policy and Practice*, 11(1): 29–47.

Kelly, P. (2006) 'What is teacher learning? A socio-cultural perspective', *Oxford Review of Education*, 32(4): 505–19.

Krovetz, M. L. and G. Arriaza (2006) *Collaborative Teacher Leadership: How Teachers Can Foster Equitable Schools*. Thousand Oaks, CA: Corwin Press.

Lave, J. and Wenger, E. (1991) *Situated Learning: Legitimate Peripheral Participation*. Cambridge: Cambridge University Press.

McIntyre, D. (2005) 'Bridging the gap between research and practice', *Cambridge Journal of Education*, 35(3): 357–82.

Moon, J. A. (2004) *Reflection in Learning and Professional Development*. London: RoutledgeFalmer.

Rickert, A. E. (1991) 'Using teacher cases for reflection and enhanced understanding', in A. Lieberman and L. Miller, *Staff Development for Education in the 90s*. New York: Teachers College Press. pp. 112–32.

Rosendahl, B. L. and K. Ronnerman (2006) 'Facilitating school improvement: the problematic relationship between researchers and practitioners', *Journal of In-service Education*, 32(4): 499–511.

Shields, P. M. (2003) 'The community of inquiry: classical pragmatism and public administration', *Administration and Society*, 35(5): 510–38.

Simons, H., Kushner, S. et al. (2003) 'From evidence-based practice to practice-based evidence: the idea of situated generalisation', *Research Papers in Education*, 18(4): 347–64.

Somekh, B. (2006) 'Constructing intercultural knowledge and understanding through collaborative action research', *Teachers and Teaching: Theory and Practice*, 12(1): 87–106.

Stenhouse, L. (1995) 'Action research and the teacher's responsibility for the educational process', in J. Rudduck and D. Hopkins, *Research as a Basis for Teaching: Readings from the Work of Lawrence Stenhouse*, London: Falmer Press.

Temperley, J. and McGrane, J. (2005) 'Enquiry in action', in H. Street and J. Temperley, *Improving Schools Through Collaborative Enquiry*. London: Continuum. pp. 72–103.

Bibliography

Alderson, P. (2000) 'School students' views on school councils and daily life at school', *Children and Society*, 14(2): 121.

Ball, D. L. and Cohen, D. K. (1999) 'Developing practice, developing practitioners: toward a practice-based theory of professional education', D. Sykes and L. Darling-Hammond, in *Teaching as the Learning Profession: Handbook of Policy and Practice*. San Francisco: Jossey Bass. pp. 3–32.

Baumfield, V., Hall, E., Higgins, S. and Wall, K. (2007) 'Tools for inquiry and the role of feedback in teachers' learning'. Paper presented at the European Association of Research into Learning and Instruction (EARLI) Conference, Budapest, September 2007.

Baumfield, V. M. and Butterworth, A. M. (2007) 'Creating and translating knowledge about teaching and learning in collaborative school/university research partnerships', *Teachers and Teaching: Theory and Practice*, 13(4). pp. 411–27.

Beijaard, et al. (2004) 'Reconsidering research on teachers' professional identity', *Teaching and Teacher Education*, 20(2): 107–28.

Bereiter, C. (2002) *Education and Mind in the Knowledge Age*. Mahwah, NJ: Lawrence Erlbaum Assoc.

Bielaczyc, K. and Collins, A. (1999) 'Learning communities in classrooms: a reconceptualization of educational practice', in C. M. Reigeluth, *Instructional-Design Theories and Models: A New Paradigm of Instructional Theory*. Mahwah, NJ: Lawrence Erlbaum. pp. 269–92.

Bryman, A. (2001) *Social Research Methods*. Oxford: Oxford University Press.

Clark, C., McQuail, S. and Moss, P. (2003) *Exploring the Field of Listening to and Consulting Young Children*. London: DfES Publications.

Clement, M. and Vandenberghe, R. (2000) 'Teachers' professional development: a solitary or collegial (ad)venture?', *Teaching and Teacher Education*, 16: 81–101.

Cochran-Smith, M. and Lytle, S. L. (2004) 'Practitioner inquiry, knowledge and university culture', in J. J. Loughran, M. L. Hamilton, V. K. LaBoskey and T. L. Russell, *International Handbook of Self-Study of Teaching and Teacher Education Practices*. Dordrecht: Kluwer Academic Publishers.

Cohen, L. and Manion, L. (1998) *Research Methods in Education*, 4th edn. London: Routledge.

Cordingley, P., Baumfield, V. M. et al. (2002) *Lessons from the School-based Research Consortia*. British Education Research Association. University of Exeter:

Cordingley, P., Bell, M., Evans, D. and Firth, A. (2005) *The Impact of Collaborative CPD on Classroom Teaching and Learning: What Do Teacher Impact Data Tell Us about Collaborative CPD?* London: EPPI-Centre.

Cordingley, P., Bell, M., Rundell, B., Evans, D. and Curtis, A. (2003) *The Impact of Collaborative CPD on Classroom Teaching and Learning: How Does Collaborative Continuing Professional Development (CPD) for Teachers of the 5–16 Age Range Affect Teaching and Learning?* London: EPPI-Centre.

Day, C., Stobart, G., Sammons, P. and Kington, A. (2006) 'Variations in the work and lives of teachers: relative and relational effectiveness', *Teachers and Teaching: Theory and Practice*, 12: 169–92.

Denscombe, M. (2003) *The Good Research Guide*, 2nd edn. Berkshire: Open University Press.

Desforges, C. and Abouchaar, A. (2003) *The Impact of Parental Involvement, Parental Support and Family Education on Pupil Achievements and Adjustment: A Literature Review*. London: Department for Education and Skills.

Ecclestone, K. (2004) 'Learning in a comfort zone: cultural and social capital inside an outcome-based assessment regime', *Assessment in Education: Principles, Policy and Practice*, 11(1): 29–47.

Flutter, J. and Ruddock, J. (2004) *Consulting Pupils: What's In It For Schools?* London: RoutledgeFalmer.

Hammersley, M. (2005) 'The myth of research based practice: the critical case of educational enquiry', *International Journal of Social Research Methodology*, 8(4): 317–30.

Harding, N. (2006) 'Ethnic and social class similarities and differences in mothers' beliefs about kindergarten preparation', *Race, Ethnicity and Education*, 9(2): 223–37.

Hargreaves, D. H. (1999) 'The knowledge-creating school', *British Journal of Educational Studies*, 47(2): 122–44.

Hattie, J. (2003) *Teachers Make a Difference: What is the Research Evidence? Distinguishing Expert Teachers from Novice and Experienced Teachers*, Australian Council for Educational Research.

HEFCE (2005) *Young Participation in Higher Education*. Available for download from http://www.hefce.ac.uk/pubs/hefce/2005/05_03/

Huberman, M. (2001) 'Networks that alter teaching: conceptualisations, exchanges and experiments', in J. Soler, A. Craft and H. Burgess, (eds), *Teacher Development – Exploring Our Own Practice*. London: Paul Chapman. pp. 141–59.

Kelly, P. (2006) 'What is teacher learning? A socio-cultural perspective', *Oxford Review of Education*, 32(4): 505–19.

Kemmis, S. and McTaggart, R. (1988) *The Action Research Planner*. Geelong: Deakin University.

Krovetz, M. L. and Arriaza, G. (2006) *Collaborative Teacher Leadership: How Teachers Can Foster Equitable Schools*. Thousand Oaks, CA: Corwin Press.

Lave, J. and Wenger, E. (1991) *Situated Learning: Legitimate Peripheral Participation*. Cambridge: Cambridge University Press.

Leat, D. (1998) *Thinking Through Geography*. Cambridge: Chris Kington Publishers.

McCallum, B., Hargreaves, E. and Gipps, C. (2000) 'Learning: the pupils' voice', *Cambridge Journal of Education*, 30(2): 275–89.

McIntyre, D. (2005) 'Bridging the gap between research and practice', *Cambridge Journal of Education*, 35(3): 357–82.

Mirza, H. S. (2006) '"Race", gender and educational desire', *Race, Ethnicity and Education*, 9(2): 137–58.

Moon, J. A. (2004) *Reflection in Learning and Professional Development*. London: RoutledgeFalmer.

Moseley, D., Baumfield, V. M., Elliott, J., Higgins, S., Miller, J., Newton, D. and Gregson, M. et al. (2005) *Frameworks for Thinking*. Cambridge: Cambridge University Press.

Ofsted (2003) *The Framework for Inspecting Schools in England from September 2003*. Available at: http://www.ofsted.gov.uk/publications/index.cfm?fuseaction=pubs.displayfile&id=1247&type=pdf (accessed 29 September 2006).

Osler, A. (2000) 'Children's rights, responsibilities and understandings of school discipline', *Research Papers in Education*, 15(1): 49–67.

Pollard, A. (1996) 'Playing the system: pupil perspectives of curriculum, assessment and pedagogy', in P. Croll (ed.), *Teachers, Pupils and Primary Schooling: Continuity and Change*. London: Cassell.

Puchta, C. and Potter, J. (2004) *Focus Group Practice*. London: Sage.

Raymond, L. (2001) 'Student involvement in school improvement: from data source to significant voice', *FORUM*, 43(2): 58–61.

Rickert, A. E. (1991) 'Using teacher cases for reflection and enhanced understanding', in A. Lieberman and L. Miller, *Staff Development for Education in the 90s*. New York: Teachers College Press. pp. 112–32.

Rosendahl, B. L. and Ronnerman, K. (2006) 'Facilitating school improvement: the problematic relationship between researchers and practitioners', *Journal of In-service Education*, 32(4): 499–511.

Sacker, A., Schoon, I., and Bartley, M. (2002) 'Social inequality in educational achievement and psychological adjustment throughout childhood: magnitude and mechanisms', *Social Science and Medicine*, 22(5): 863–80.

Shields, P. M. (2003) 'The Community of inquiry: classical pragmatism and public administration'. *Administration and Society*, 35(5): 510–38.

Simon, B. (1999) 'Why no pedagogy in England?', in J. Leach and B. Moon (eds), *Learners and Pedagogy*. London: Paul Chapman/Open University. pp. 34–45.

Simons, H., Kushner, S. Jones, K. and James, D. (2003) 'From evidence-based practice to practice-based evidence: the idea of situated generalisation', *Research Papers in Education*, 18(4): 347–64.

Smith, H. and Higgins, S. E. (2006) 'Opening classroom interaction: the importance of feedback', *Cambridge Journal of Education*, 36(4): 485–502.

Somekh, B. (2006) 'Constructing intercultural knowledge and understanding through collaborative action research', *Teachers and Teaching: Theory and Practice* 12(1): 87–106.

Stenhouse, L. (1981) 'What counts as research?' *British Journal of Educational Studies*, 29(2): 103–14.

Stenhouse, L. (1995) 'Action research and the teacher's responsibility for the educational process', in J. Rudduck and D. Hopkins, *Research as a Basis for Teaching: Readings from the Work of Lawrence Stenhouse*. London: Falmer Press.

Temperley, J. and McGrane, J. (2005) 'Enquiry in action', in H. Street and J. Temperley, *Improving Schools Through Collaborative Enquiry*. London: Continuum. pp. 72–103.

Thomas, S., Smees, R. and Boyd, B. (1998) *Valuing Pupil Views in Scottish Schools,* Policy Paper No. 3, The Improving School Effectiveness Project. London: Institute of Education.

Training and Development Agency (2006) *Draft Revised Standards for Classroom Teachers*. London: Training and Development Agency.

Tunstall, P. and Gipps, C. (1996) 'Teacher feedback to young children in formative assessment: a typology', *British Educational Research Journal*, 22: 389–404.

United Nations Convention on the Rights of the Child (1989) *UN General Assembly Resolution 44/25*. Available online at: www.unhchr.ch/html/ menu3/ b/k2crc (accessed 12 June 2005).

Vygotsky, L. S. (1978) *Mind in Society: The Development of Higher Psychological Processes*. Cambridge, MA: Harvard University Press.

Osler, A. (2000) 'Children's rights, responsibilities and understandings of school discipline', *Research Papers in Education*, 15(1): 49–67.

Pollard, A. (1996) 'Playing the system: pupil perspectives of curriculum, assessment and pedagogy', in P. Croll (ed.), *Teachers, Pupils and Primary Schooling: Continuity and Change*. London: Cassell.

Puchta, C. and Potter, J. (2004) *Focus Group Practice*. London: Sage.

Raymond, L. (2001) 'Student involvement in school improvement: from data source to significant voice', *FORUM*, 43(2): 58–61.

Rickert, A. E. (1991) 'Using teacher cases for reflection and enhanced understanding', in A. Lieberman and L. Miller, *Staff Development for Education in the 90s*. New York: Teachers College Press. pp. 112–32.

Rosendahl, B. L. and Ronnerman, K. (2006) 'Facilitating school improvement: the problematic relationship between researchers and practitioners', *Journal of In-service Education*, 32(4): 499–511.

Sacker, A., Schoon, I., and Bartley, M. (2002) 'Social inequality in educational achievement and psychological adjustment throughout childhood: magnitude and mechanisms', *Social Science and Medicine*, 22(5): 863–80.

Shields, P. M. (2003) 'The Community of inquiry: classical pragmatism and public administration'. *Administration and Society*, 35(5): 510–38.

Simon, B. (1999) 'Why no pedagogy in England?', in J. Leach and B. Moon (eds), *Learners and Pedagogy*. London: Paul Chapman/Open University. pp. 34–45.

Simons, H., Kushner, S. Jones, K. and James, D. (2003) 'From evidence-based practice to practice-based evidence: the idea of situated generalisation', *Research Papers in Education*, 18(4): 347–64.

Smith, H. and Higgins, S. E. (2006) 'Opening classroom interaction: the importance of feedback', *Cambridge Journal of Education*, 36(4): 485–502.

Somekh, B. (2006) 'Constructing intercultural knowledge and understanding through collaborative action research', *Teachers and Teaching: Theory and Practice* 12(1): 87–106.

Stenhouse, L. (1981) 'What counts as research?' *British Journal of Educational Studies*, 29(2): 103–14.

Stenhouse, L. (1995) 'Action research and the teacher's responsibility for the educational process', in J. Rudduck and D. Hopkins, *Research as a Basis for Teaching: Readings from the Work of Lawrence Stenhouse*. London: Falmer Press.

Temperley, J. and McGrane, J. (2005) 'Enquiry in action', in H. Street and J. Temperley, *Improving Schools Through Collaborative Enquiry*. London: Continuum. pp. 72–103.

Thomas, S., Smees, R. and Boyd, B. (1998) *Valuing Pupil Views in Scottish Schools*, Policy Paper No. 3, The Improving School Effectiveness Project. London: Institute of Education.

Training and Development Agency (2006) *Draft Revised Standards for Classroom Teachers*. London: Training and Development Agency.

Tunstall, P. and Gipps, C. (1996) 'Teacher feedback to young children in formative assessment: a typology', *British Educational Research Journal*, 22: 389–404.

United Nations Convention on the Rights of the Child (1989) *UN General Assembly Resolution 44/25*. Available online at: www.unhchr.ch/html/ menu3/ b/k2crc (accessed 12 June 2005).

Vygotsky, L. S. (1978) *Mind in Society: The Development of Higher Psychological Processes*. Cambridge, MA: Harvard University Press.

Wall, K. and Higgins, S. (2006) 'Facilitating and supporting talk with pupils about metacognition: a research and learning tool, *International Journal of Research and Methods in Education*, 29(1): 39–53.

Wien, C. A. (1995) *Developmentally Appropriate Practice in 'Real Life': Stories of Teacher Practical Knowledge*. New York: Teachers College Press.

Worrall, S. (2000) *Young People as Researchers: A Learning Resource Pack*. London: Save the Children/Joseph Rowntree Foundation.

Wragg, E. and Woo, E. K. (1984) 'Teachers' first encounters with their classes', in E. Wragg (ed.), *Classroom Teaching Skills*. London: Croom Helm.

Index